ISBN 0-8373-0196-3

C-196 CAREER EXAMINATION SERIES

This is your PASSBOOK® for...

Dietitian

Test Preparation Study Guide

Questions & Answers

EAST NORTHPORT PUBLIC LIBRARY
EAST NORTHPORT, NEW YORK

NATIONAL LEARNING CORPORATION

Copyright © 2014 by

National Learning Corporation

212 Michael Drive, Syosset, New York 11791

All rights reserved, including the right of reproduction in whole or in part, in any form or by any means, electronic or mechanical, including photocopying, recording, or by any information storage and retrieval system, without permission in writing from the Publisher.

(516) 921-8888
(800) 645-6337
FAX: (516) 921-8743
www.passbooks.com
sales @ passbooks.com
info @ passbooks.com

PRINTED IN THE UNITED STATES OF AMERICA

PASSBOOK®

NOTICE

This book is SOLELY intended for, is sold ONLY to, and its use is RESTRICTED to *individual*, bona fide applicants or candidates who qualify by virtue of having seriously filed applications for appropriate license, certificate, professional and/or promotional advancement, higher school matriculation, scholarship, or other legitimate requirements of educational and/or governmental authorities.

This book is NOT intended for use, class instruction, tutoring, training, duplication, copying, reprinting, excerption, or adaptation, etc., by:

(1) Other publishers

(2) Proprietors and/or Instructors of "Coaching" and/or Preparatory Courses

(3) Personnel and/or Training Divisions of commercial, industrial, and governmental organizations

(4) Schools, colleges, or universities and/or their departments and staffs, including teachers and other personnel

(5) Testing Agencies or Bureaus

(6) Study groups which seek by the purchase of a single volume to copy and/or duplicate and/or adapt this material for use by the group as a whole without having purchased individual volumes for each of the members of the group

(7) Et al.

Such persons would be in violation of appropriate Federal and State statutes.

PROVISION OF LICENSING AGREEMENTS. — Recognized educational commercial, industrial, and governmental institutions and organizations, and others legitimately engaged in educational pursuits, including training, testing, and measurement activities, may address a request for a licensing agreement to the copyright owners, who will determine whether, and under what conditions, including fees and charges, the materials in this book may be used by them. In other words, a licensing facility exists for the legitimate use of the material in this book on other than an individual basis. However, it is asseverated and affirmed here that the material in this book *CANNOT* be used without the receipt of the express permission of such a licensing agreement from the Publishers.

NATIONAL LEARNING CORPORATION
212 Michael Drive
Syosset, New York 11791

Inquiries re licensing agreements should be addressed to:
The President
National Learning Corporation
212 Michael Drive
Syosset, New York 11791

PASSBOOK® SERIES

THE *PASSBOOK® SERIES* has been created to prepare applicants and candidates for the ultimate academic battlefield — the examination room.

At some time in our lives, each and every one of us may be required to take an examination — for validation, matriculation, admission, qualification, registration, certification, or licensure.

Based on the assumption that every applicant or candidate has met the basic formal educational standards, has taken the required number of courses, and read the necessary texts, the *PASSBOOK® SERIES* furnishes the one special preparation which may assure passing with confidence, instead of failing with insecurity. Examination questions — together with answers — are furnished as the basic vehicle for study so that the mysteries of the examination and its compounding difficulties may be eliminated or diminished by a sure method.

This book is meant to help you pass your examination provided that you qualify and are serious in your objective.

The entire field is reviewed through the huge store of content information which is succinctly presented through a provocative and challenging approach — the question-and-answer method.

A climate of success is established by furnishing the correct answers at the end of each test.

You soon learn to recognize types of questions, forms of questions, and patterns of questioning. You may even begin to anticipate expected outcomes.

You perceive that many questions are repeated or adapted so that you can gain acute insights, which may enable you to score many sure points.

You learn how to confront new questions, or types of questions, and to attack them confidently and work out the correct answers.

You note objectives and emphases, and recognize pitfalls and dangers, so that you may make positive educational adjustments.

Moreover, you are kept fully informed in relation to new concepts, methods, practices, and directions in the field.

You discover that you are actually taking the examination all the time: you are preparing for the examination by "taking" an examination, not by reading extraneous and/or supererogatory textbooks.

In short, this PASSBOOK®, used directedly, should be an important factor in helping you to pass your test.

DIETITIAN

DUTIES:

Assists in the preparation of menus and special diets; supervises subordinate food service personnel in the preparation and serving of food to patients in a general hospital or institution;

Dietitian under supervision, assist in the operation of a food and/or nutrition service of an institution or hospital; make nutritional assessments; interview clients and/or their families to obtain history of food habits and preferences; explain diet to clients and/or families and monitor reaction to diet; interpret laboratory, physical and social data in medical records; monitor clients for and evaluate food/drug interactions; consult physicians about appropriate menu modifications; assist with preparation of nutritional analysis of general and therapeutic cycle menus; prepare client nutritional care plans; participate in testing new recipes and report results for possible inclusion in department recipe manual; supervise the receipt, storage and distribution of food and other supplies; participate in nutritional training of field placement students; participate in rounds with patient health care team; maintain liaison with community organizations relating to nutrition education and/or information; may participate in nutritional community health fairs; maintain records and writes reports;

Under general supervision, an employee in this class assesses nutritional needs, and develops and implements diets to meet the nutritional needs of the client population. this is professional work requiring overall menu development to meet the dietary needs of senior citizens, participants in the WIC program or patients included in this may be the need to develop therapeutic or specialized diets; the incumbent coordinates clinical and administrative aspects of dietetics to provide appropriate care and services; work is reviewed by an administrative supervisor through observations and staff conferences; supervision is exercised over food service personnel. Does related work as required.

SCOPE OF THE EXAMINATION:

The written test designed to evaluate knowledge, skills and /or abilities in the following areas:

1. Food preparation and service programs;
2. Advanced nutrition and dietetics;
3. Patient/client dietary care;
4. Public contact principles and practices; and
5. Supervision.

DIETITIANS

NATURE OF THE WORK

Dietitians plan nutritious and appetizing meals to help people maintain or recover good health. They also supervise the food service workers who prepare and serve the meals, manage purchases and keep the accounts, and give advice on good eating habits. Administrative dietitians form the largest group in this occupation; the others are clinical, teaching, and research dietitians. Nutritionists also are included in this field.

Administrative dietitians apply the principles of nutrition and sound management to large-scale meal planning and preparation, such as that done in hospitals, universities, schools, and other institutions. They supervise the planning, preparation, and service of meals; select, train, and direct food-service supervisors and workers; budget for and purchase food, equipment, and supplies; enforce sanitary and safety regulations; and prepare records and reports. Dietitians who are directors of a dietetic department also decide on departmental policy; coordinate dietetic service with the activities of other departments; and are responsible for the development and management of the dietetic department budget, which in large organizations may amount to millions of dollars annually.

Clinical dietitians, sometimes called therapeutic dietitians, plan diets and supervise the service of meals to meet the nutritional needs of patients in hospitals, nursing homes, or clinics. Among their duties, clinical dietitians confer with doctors and other members of the health-care team about the patients' nutritional care, instruct patients and their families on the requirements and importance of their diets, and suggest ways to help them stay on these diets after leaving the hospital or clinic. In a small institution, one person may be both the administrative and clinical dietitian.

Research dietitians evaluate and interpret research findings to improve the nutrition of people in health and in disease. This research may be in nutrition science and education, food management, food service systems and equipment. They conduct studies and make surveys of food intake, food acceptance, and food utilization in the body for individuals and groups of people. Research projects may relate to subjects such as nutritional needs of the aging, persons with a chronic disease, or space travelers.

Dietetic educators teach normal nutrition and nutrition in disease to dietetic, medical, dental, and nursing students and to interns, residents, and other members of the health-care team. This may be in hospitals, clinics, and schools.

Nutritionists counsel people of all ages, as individuals or in groups, on sound nutrition practices, to maintain and improve health. This includes food budgeting and purchasing, and meal planning and preparation. Nutritionists in the public health field are responsible for planning, developing, administering, and coordinating nutrition programs and services as part of public health programs.

An increasing number of dietitians work as consultants to hospitals and to health-related facilities. Others act as consultants to commercial enterprises, including food processors, equipment manufacturers, and utility companies.

PLACES OF EMPLOYMENT

About 100,000 persons, most of them women, work as dietitians. More than two-fifths work in hospitals and clinics, including about 5,000 in the Veterans Administration and the United States Public Health Service. Colleges, universities, and school systems employ a large number of dietitians as teachers or as dietitians in food service systems. Most of the rest work for public health agencies, restaurants, or cafeterias and large companies that provide food service for their employees. Some dietitians are commissioned officers in the Armed Forces.

TRAINING, OTHER QUALIFICATIONS, AND ADVANCEMENT

A bachelor's degree, preferably with a major in foods and nutrition or institution management, is the basic educational requirement for dietitians. This degree can be earned in more than 250 colleges and universities, usually in departments of home economics. College courses usually required are in food and nutrition, institution management, chemistry, bacteriology, physiology, and related courses such as mathematics, data processing, psychology, sociology, and economics.

For a dietitian to qualify for professional recognition, the Academy of Nutrition and Dietetics, formerly known as the American Dietetic Association, recommends the completion after graduation of an approved dietetic internship or 2 years' experience. Seventy-five internship programs were approved by the American Dietetic Association. A growing number of coordinated undergraduate programs, located in schools of medicine and in allied health and home economics departments of both colleges and universities, enable students to complete both the requirements for a bachelor's degree and the clinical experience requirement in four years.

Experienced dietitians may advance to assistant director or director of a dietetic department in a large hospital or other institution. Advancement to higher level positions in teaching and research usually requires graduate education; public health nutritionists must earn a graduate degree in this field. Graduate study in institutional or business administration is valuable to those interested in administrative dietetics.

Persons who plan to become dietitians should have organizational and administrative ability, as well as high scientific aptitude, and should be able to work well with a variety of people.

EMPLOYMENT OUTLOOK

Employment opportunities for qualified dietitians on both a full-time and part-time basis are expected to continue to be good. In recent years, dietetic assistants trained in vocational and technical schools and dietetic technicians trained in junior colleges have increasingly been utilized by employers to help meet demands for dietetic services. Since this situation is likely to persist, employment opportunities also should continue to be favorable for graduates of these programs.

Employment of dietitians is expected to grow rapidly to meet the nutrition and food management needs of hospitals and extended care facilities, schools, industrial plants, and restaurants. Dietitians also will be needed to staff community health programs and to conduct research in food and nutrition. In addition to new dietitians needed because of occupational growth, many others will be required each year to replace those who die, retire, or leave the profession for marriage and family responsibilities.

The number of men dietitians is growing. Men are likely to find increasing employment opportunities, especially as administrative dietitians in college and university food services, hospitals, and commercial eating places.

WORKING CONDITIONS

Most dietitians work 40 hours a week; however, dietitians in hospitals may sometimes work on weekends, and those in commercial food service have somewhat irregular hours. Some hospitals provide laundry service and meals in addition to salary. Dietitians usually receive paid vacations, holidays, and health insurance and retirement benefits.

SOURCES OF ADDITIONAL INFORMATION

For information on approved dietetic internship programs, scholarships, and employment opportunities, and a list of colleges providing training for a professional career in dietetics, contact:

Academy of Nutrition and Dietetics
120 South Riverside Plaza, Suite 2000
Chicago, Illinois 60606-1600

DIETETICS AND NUTRITION

CAREER DESCRIPTIONS

CONTENTS

		Page
I.	Dietetic Assistant	1
II.	Dietetic Technician	2
III.	Dietitian	3
IV.	Food Technologist	5
V.	Home Economist	7

DIETETICS AND NUTRITION

CAREER DESCRIPTIONS

Human nutrition is the science of food and its effect on the human body. It is concerned with the nutrients in food, their use in body chemistry and physiology, and, in the final analysis, with the wide range of relationships of foods to maintaining or restoring health.

In this field, the term "nutritionist" is a general occupational title which applies to different types of health professionals involved with food science and human nutrition. Among these professionals are the dietitian, food technologist, and home economist, and each of these careers is discussed in depth in the following pages. In addition, career information about dietetic technicians and dietetic assistants engaged in food administration and nutrition services is presented in detail in this section.

I. Dietetic Assistant

**Dietetic service supervisor
Food-service supervisor**

Dietetic assistants work under the direction of a dietitian or dietetic technician and are responsible for supervising food services and nutrition-care services in various types of facilities. Their duties depend in large part on the size, type, and organization of the facility. Typical responsibilities in food-services activities include assisting with menu planning, production schedules, and the standardization of recipes. In addition, assistants oversee the ordering, receiving, and storing of food and supplies; supervise various dietary workers; and maintain sanitation, safety, and security practices. In health-care facilities, patient-care services involve dietetic assistants in such tasks as processing dietary orders, menus, and other related directives; helping patients with menu selection; and writing routine modified diets according to established patterns.

Dietetic assistants also instruct and train dietary workers in the use, care, and maintenance of equipment and assist in orientation, on-the-job training, and in-service educational programs for dietary personnel. Added duties include recommending improvements in facilities and equipment, suggesting changes in policies and procedures, and evaluating the work performance of subordinates.

In addition to the dietetic assistant, there are other workers who provide important supportive services in dietetics and nutrition. Two of these are the dietetic clerical worker and the dietetic worker.

In general, the dietetic clerical worker assists the dietitian with paperwork—and there is a great deal of it in a dietetics department. In addition to general secretarial and clerical duties, this also includes typing menus, purchase orders, and recipes; tallying food supplies issued to the cooks; preparing worksheets; calculating recipe and menu costs; and the many similar office tasks involved in large-scale food service. No special training is required beyond basic stenographic and clerical skills of the kind taught in a high school business course.

It takes a good-sized staff to run any large-scale food service. The number of people required and the extent to which each one specializes in just one part of the operation depend on the size of the facility or organization. But, whether the institution is large or small, the jobs that need doing cover the whole range of food preparation—storing, preparing, cooking, and serving, as well as dishwashing and kitchen cleaning. Every one of these jobs performed by the dietetic worker is an important link in maintaining high standards. Training is usually given on the job. However, courses may be taken in vocational high schools to prepare students and adults for food service employment. For employees who show interest and aptitude, classes under a dietitian may be offered in such subjects as nutrition, food preparation, storage, and sanitation. With experience, it is possible to qualify for positions of greater responsibility.

Dietetic assistants and other dietary employees work in a variety of organizations including hospitals, nursing-care facilities, schools, day- and geriatric-care centers, and in industrial food-service establishments. Assistants usually work a 40-hour week, which may involve weekends, and do considerable amounts of standing and walking during normal perforance of duties.

Job Requirements

Career preparation includes a high school diploma or the equivalent, plus completion of an approved program in food management and dietetics leading to a dietetic assistant certificate. These programs are offered in community colleges or postsecondary technical schools and consist of academic and clinical components, including supervised field experience. Programs generally last about 1 year and are approved by the American Dietetic Association. In addition to vocational training, candidates should have supervisory potential, an interest in working with food, and the ability to work well with people.

Dietetics and Nutrition

Opportunities

Employment opportunities for dietetic assistants and other dietary employees are quite favorable. This is due to the increasing use of trained assistants and dietary workers to meet expanded demands for dietetic and nutrition services by health facilities, educational institutions, food-service systems, and various other organizations. Dietetic assistants can advance to dietetic technician or dietitian by successfully completing additional academic and supervised clinical training.

For further information, contact:
The American Dietetic Association

technicians work a 40-hour week, and, depending on the type of establishment, may be required to work weekends.

Job Requirements

An individual considering this career should be a high school graduate with an appreciation of quality food, an interest in people, and the potential to develop basic management skills. The basic vocational preparation for the career of dietetic technician consists of an associate-degree program for dietetic technicians in an accredited junior or community college which combines classroom studies with practical instruction in this field under actual working conditions.

II. Dietetic Technician

Dietetic technicians are members of the dietary staff who specialize in food administration and/or nutrition-care services. Specialists in food administration perform a variety of tasks including producing quality food, developing standardized recipes, managing cafeterias, and the training of personnel. The size and organization of the department of dietetics in the facility determines the exact nature of the technicians' duties. For example, in a large hospital dietetic technicians work under the supervision of a dietitian, while in a small hospital or related health facility they may assume responsibility for total food service under the supervision of an administrator and a consultant dietitian. Technicians in food-service management may also be responsible for budget control, employee and production scheduling, sanitation, and safety, security standards, and controls.

Technicians who specialize in nutrition-care work under the supervision of a clinical or community dietitian. Typical duties include taking diet histories, calculating routine modified diets, teaching patients normal nutritional habits, and visiting patients to evaluate their food programs. Some technicians work in community programs teaching low-income families the economics of food purchasing, preparation, and nutrition. They also direct food services, day-care centers, and assist nationals of other countries in adapting menu patterns and in purchasing and preparing nutritious foods.

Dietetic technicians are employed in a variety of organizations. These include hospitals, medical centers, nursing-care facilities, child- and geriatric-care centers, headstart programs, youth centers, schools, clinics and industrial-food-service establishments. Usually

Opportunities

There are increasing employment opportunities for dietetic technicians, due primarily to a greater emphasis on health care and nutrition throughout the country. However, technicians should be willing to look beyond local labor markets if the area nearest their training institution becomes oversupplied and there is increased competition for available openings. Dietetic technicians may advance to positions as dietitians by completing an approved undergraduate program leading to a degree in dietetics, nutrition, home economics, food science, or food-service management.

For further information, contact:
The American Dietetic Association

III. Dietitian

Dietitians are professionals who provide nutritional care to individuals and groups and apply the principles of management to food service systems. They promote sound nutritional practices to promote good health and to treat disease and assist in the rehabilitation of individuals through applied principles of nutrition and education. There are five major areas in dietetics—administration, clinical, education, community, and research—and within these areas are specializations.

Administrative dietitians are specialists in food service systems and are members of the management team. They apply their skills to maintain optimum efficiency in quality food production and service in providing nutritional care to individuals and groups. Administrative dietitians develop menu patterns and evaluate their acceptance. They develop specifications for the procurement of food, equipment, and supplies and establish and maintain standards for sanitation, safety, and security. Administrative dietitians are involved in all phases of personnel management including planning, conducting, and evaluating orientation and in-service educational programs. They are in demand in hospitals and other health-related facilities as well as in food service in schools, universities, industry, hotels, restaurants, and other commercial organizations.

A successful experienced administrative dietitian may become a director of a department of dietetics in a hospital-related health facility or other type of organization with a department of dietetics or nutrition. In the hospital, the director assumes the responsibility of management for all food service systems serving patients and personnel. Directors develop short- and long-range goals for the department as well as manage and control fiscal resources and budget programs. They insure that all department services are coordinated within and with other departments.

Clinical dietitians, sometimes called therapeutic, specialize in the nutritional care of patients in a hospital, clinic, or other health facility. Clinical dietitians develop and implement plans based on the nutritional assessment of patients. They confer with physicians and other members of the health team and correlate the patient's nutritional care plan with other patient care plans. They provide nutritional care for all patients and plan modified diets and supervise their service. They evaluate and followup on patients' nutritional care programs and record all necessary data on the patients' medical charts. Clinical dietitians also

provide for the nutritional education of patients and families and serve as advisors on nutritional care to all members of the health-care team.

Consultant dietitians may provide advice or services in nutritional care and/or in management of food service systems in hospitals, clinics, and other health-related facilities. These experienced dietitians usually have backgrounds in clinical dietetics and in management of food service systems. They evaluate and monitor all aspects of the food service operation and make recommendations to insure the provision of nutritionally adequate quality food. Consultant dietitians may plan, organize, and conduct training programs for food service personnel, develop menu patterns, and consult with members of the health team.

Community dietitians are members of the community health team. They assess the nutritional needs of individuals and groups and develop menu patterns suited to their particular needs. These dietitians develop and implement plans of care based on an assessment of nutritional needs and other health care plans in effect. They instruct individuals and families in nutritional principles, diet food selection, preparation, and economics and adapt teaching to individual lifestyles of clients. Other community dietitians take part in evaluating dietary studies in surveys and participating in nutritional and epidemiologic studies with a nutritional component. Community dietitians work mainly in government and voluntary health agencies concerned with health and with the nutritional component of health-care services to individuals and groups.

Research dietitians participate in planning, organizing, and conducting programs in one or more of the following areas: nutrition, foods, and food service systems research. They analyze recent scientific discoveries applicable in their fields and apply them to current research. They interpret their findings to health professionals and the public and communicate through reports and publications. They may plan, conduct, and evaluate dietary studies and participate in epidemiologic studies with a nutritional component. Research dietitians may be employed in a medical center, educational institution, or commercial enterprise or may be involved in a community health program.

A specialization attracting an increasing number of experienced dietitians is that of private practice. These dietitians are self-employed and may provide nutrition consultation to a variety of clients. Others engage in practice with physicians whose patients need nutritional guidance and some are consultant dietitians providing services to small hospitals and health-related facilities.

The majority of dietitians work in hospitals, related health facilities, and clinics. Others are employed in voluntary health agencies as well as in local, State, Federal health agencies; all branches of the military; colleges, universities, and school systems; day-care centers; industrial food service; restaurants; and research institutions.

Dietitians, particularly those in hospitals and related health facilities, work closely with people, both sick and well, of all ages and backgrounds. They have frequent contact with patients, clients, and their families, as well as other health professionals and departmental personnel. In hospital and clinical settings, dietitians may spend considerable time standing and walking. They work approximately 40 hours per week

and may work occasional weekends and holidays. Contact with people physical demands, and working hours vary with specialization and type of employment.

Job Requirements

Students considering careers in dietetics should have an interest in food and its preparation; a desire to teach and share knowledge with others; and a special aptitude for the sciences related to food. The basic educational requirement for this career is a bachelor's degree in dietetics, nutrition, home economics, food science, or food service management. An increasing number of universities offer programs which prepare graduates for beginning positions. However, most graduates enroll in a dietetic internship accredited by the American Dietetic Association (ADA). The internship lasts 6 to 12 months and provides an educational program of clinical experience (under the supervision of a registered dietitian) plus classroom work. Several universities offer an 18-month program which combines the dietetic internship and graduate study leading to a master's degree.

The basic undergraduate programs in this field consist of studies in the physical, biological, and behavioral sciences, with emphasis on the field of human nutrition. Subject matter includes food and ecology management; time-money-human resources; statistics and data processing; chemistry of food; biochemistry and human nutrition, and human physiology; behavioral sciences and the processes of change; and the health-team approach to preventing and treating disease.

Dietitians who meet certain academic and experience requirements are eligible to join the American Dietetic Association. Membership is considered important because it provides evidence that the individual has met high qualification standards. The designation RD (registered dietitian) is given to those who meet certain academic and experience requirements and may be used by members who pass an examination and maintain a given number of hours in continuing education every 5 years.

Opportunities

Employment prospects for qualified dietitians are expected to be favorable during the next decade. This outlook is based on anticipated increases in demand by all types of health facilities, community health programs, educational institutions, and research organizations to meet their nutrition and food-management needs.

Opportunities for advancement in this field are generally good. For example, with experience and a master's degree come opportunities for advancement to a position as director of a department of dietetics. Dietitians who are planning a career in public health must complete a graduate degree in public health nutrition in preparation for promotion.

For further information, contact:
The American Dietetic Association

IV.

Food Technologist

**Food engineer
Food scientist**

Food technologists play a key role in developing and processing the enormous variety of foods available today. They apply scientific and engineering skills to the production, processing, packaging, distribution, preparation, evaluation, and utilization of all types of foods. They employ their specialized knowledge to solve technological problems associated with the development of products, processes, or equipment; the selection of raw materials; the fundamental changes in the physical and chemical condition of food undergoing industrial processing; or the nutritional value of such foods and their suitability for human consumption.

Depending on where they work and the size of the organization, food technologists are involved in a variety of functions. Those who work in food manufacturing, for example, develop entirely new types of food from unusual or previously unused sources. Technologists working in processing are concerned with quality control and investigation of changes occurring in foods when they are processed and stored. Technologists employed in quality control laboratories conduct chemical tests on raw materials, food composition, and additives to assure purity, safety, and accuracy in labeling. They also use various instruments to check the physical properties of the product for such factors as product softness, color, and required warehousing conditions.

Food technologists may engage in pilot testing when a new product or process leaves the laboratory and is ready to go into full production. Using equipment and machinery patterned after those used in production, but built on a smaller scale, food technologists experiment with production techniques until they find a practical routine that can be put to use by other food technologists. This may require constructing a new plant, designing and laying out equipment and machinery, and planning the work flow. Other duties of food technologists include selecting raw materials, setting specifications for additives and ingredients, findings uses for by-product materials, supervising plant sanitation and waste controls, and studying and improving the nutritive and dietary values of food products.

About 75 percent of all food technologists are employed by food manufacturers and food processing plants, while the other 25 percent work in Government,

Dietetics and Nutrition

education, and research. In Government, technologists may be employed by regulatory agencies, such as the Food and Drug Administration (FDA), the Environmental Protection Agency (EPA), and their counterparts at the local and State levels. Other Government departments using food technologists include the Department of Defense, Department of Commerce, Department of Agriculture, and the State Department. At the international level, technologists are employed by the Food and Agricultural Organization (WHO) of the United Nations. In the field of education, food technologists engage in teaching and/or research in major colleges, universities, and educational and health foundations. They also teach in community and junior colleges offering 2-year associate degree programs for food technicians. Some food technologists choose to work in sales and marketing, selling equipment or ingredients tailored to a food processor's needs, while others enter the related fields of advertising, technical editing, publishing, patent law, and private consulting.

Working conditions in food technology depend in large part on the type of organization. For example, technologists in industrial quality control and research and development laboratories work in well-equipped, clean, air-conditioned environments. However, when their work takes them from the laboratory to other areas of the industrial plant, they are subject to the hazards of occasional food spills and wet floors. Most industrial plants, including food manfacturing and processing plants, have noisy operating machinery and equipment.

Regardless of where these specialists are employed, the health forces of the Nation look to food technologists to safeguard our food and to help develop more healthful, varied, and abundant foods for more and more people.

Job Requirements

A bachelor's degree in food science or in a related science such as chemistry, biochemistry, microbiology, bacteriology, or in food engineering is the minimum educational requirement for entrance into this field. The kinds of training available in this field vary widely, and persons considering this career area should gather as much information as possible from the approximately 60 schools offering programs in this specialty. Some colleges, for example, do not have a separate department of food technology while others offer programs leading to a bachelor's degree but no further. A few may have only a graduate program leading to a master's or a doctor's degree.

Whatever college is selected, the first 2 years should include courses in such basic science subjects as chemistry, bacteriology, physics, nutrition, biology, and mathematics. In fact, the whole program should give a thorough understanding of the fundamentals of science, engineering, and agriculture, together with their application to the manufacturing and processing of foods. A master's or doctoral degree is highly desirable for many careers in industry, and it is a necessity for careers in teaching or research.

There are no licensure or certification requirements for this work. However, membership in the Institute of Food Technologists is available to all individuals in the field with a B.S. or advanced degree in food technology of food science (or a related field), and those with 5 years of professional experience may achieve Professional Member status.

Opportunities

Employment opportunities for food technologists are expected to grow during the next decade. The food industry is one of the largest and most stable industries in the United States, and the demand for new, quality foods which are easy to prepare, package, store, and distribute is steadily increasing. In addition, the skills of the food technologist are needed in research and development activities dealing with such problems as feeding the poor in underdeveloped countries and creating special foods for use in space and underwater programs.

A career in food technology is challenging from a scientific viewpoint, and, although beginning jobs may be routine, the advancement opportunities for qualified workers are excellent. A technologist often begins as a food chemist in the research and development laboratory of an industrial plant and, after gaining added experience and education, is able to advance to

such positions as senior technologist, group leader, assistant research director, or research director. Some technologists start work in the production department of a food company and, when qualified, move into management positions such as production or quality control supervisor, section or division chief, assistant director or manager of quality control, or plant manager. Technologists with advanced degrees often begin their careers in teaching or research activities and advance through the traditional methods employed by most educational institutions. Frequently, food technologists with interests in business enter fields such as sales or marketing and ultimately may qualify for high-level management positions. In general, food technologists with advanced degrees in food science have greater employment opportunities than those at the bachelor's degree level, or those with degrees in related fields such as chemistry or microbiology.

For further information, contact: Institute of Food Technologists

V. Home Economist

Home economists develop, interpret, and apply a broad knowledge of homemaking principles to promote the health and welfare of individuals and families. They focus on family functions and the effect of economic, social, cultural, and psychological forces on the family and its members. In doing so, they use knowledge not only from their own field but also from the biological, physical, and social sciences as well as the arts. Some home economists are specialists in areas such as food and nutrition, family economics, home management, child development, and family relations, while others are generalists.

Home economists in the health field perform vital functions in dealing with a variety of family-related problems. Their broad responsibilities include providing individuals and families with advice on family economics, home management, and consumer education. Specifically, home economists teach improved homemaking practices to homemakers and young people through educational programs, demonstrations, discussions, and home visits. They provide families with help in preparing budgets as well as advice on managing time and other resources. Home economists also work with mentally retarded individuals to help them develop home-management and child-care abilities. They engage in research in government agencies, colleges, and universities to gather new data on family relations or child development, or to discover facts on food or nutrition.

There are many opportunities for the home economist in rehabilitation. The woman who is recovering from a heart attack or tuberculosis, for example, may not be able to climb stairs or do the other activities that were previously routine. Similarly, persons who are confined to wheelchairs and can no longer use their hands skillfully, or are limited to one hand, will find it impossible to manage in the same old way. Either new ways must be learned to carry out these everyday activities or someone else must take them over.

Men, too, need the help of the home economist in home management, family finance, nutrition, and other home-related areas. For men who live alone, learning to manage for one's self around the house can be an important element in convalescence or in adjusting to a permanent disability. There are men who have disabilities which make it impossible for them to be employed outside the home. If they could assume housekeeping responsibilities, it would release other family members for outside employment.

In addition, many older people enfeebled by age might continue to live independently in their homes for many years if they could be helped to simplify their homemaking and make it less strenuous.

Handicapped children and young people who have been retrained in homemaking could assume an active role in the family, reducing the burden of the parents.

The duties of the home economist in rehabilitation vary, but they can be classified into two categories: direct counseling of the handicapped individual and indirect counseling as a resource person for the rehabilitation team.

The home economist in rehabilitation may offer many different types of help:

- Suggest work plans and management practices to save time and energy.
- Plan kitchen arrangements to make the work easier.
- Assist a patient with a physical handicap (such as blindness or loss of a limb) to perform household duties in a way which will get around the handicap.
- Help patients with difficulty in body control and coordination to develop correct postures and positions.

In the rehabilitation movement as a whole, there is a growing demand for specialists with home economics background and training in occupational therapy to serve as resource persons for the rehabilitation team.

On a full-time basis, specialists often assist with staff training programs, provide service materials, and contribute to research. Acting as a resource consultant, the home economist in rehabilitation provides the rehabilitation team with answers to problems of management, with special emphasis on such areas as work simplification, nutrition and food preparation, adaptations of clothing, child care, family relations, furnishings, and interior design.

Home economists are employed by rehabilitation centers; hospitals; convalescent centers; Federal, State and local agencies; the Cooperative Extension Service; secondary schools; colleges; universities; research laboratories; private business firms; and social welfare agencies. They generally work 40 hours per week, and the physical demands and working conditions vary according to the type of establishment in which they are employed.

Job Requirements

A bachelor's degree in home economics is the basic educational requirement for entry into this field. While in high school, students considering this career are urged to take courses in speech, English, home economics, health, mathematics, chemistry, and social sciences in preparation for college work. Individuals planning a career in this field should have good communication skills and be able to work effectively with individuals from different cultures and income levels.

The background required for home economists in rehabilitation is more extensive. The primary educational requisite for a home economist in rehabilitation is a 4-year college education with emphasis in one or more of these areas: home economics, occupational therapy, or social work. A qualified home economist in rehabilitation should have graduate or in-service training in the special education of the orthopedically handicapped, blind, deaf, cardiac, retarded, or mentally ill. If planning to work in a hospital, the consultant should have some hospital in-service training and orientation.

Prior professional work experience may include one of the following: occupational therapy, physical therapy, dietetics or nutrition, hospital or public health nursing, social work, or home economics.

Practical experience in homemaking and child care is

extremely important. The consultant should have a clear picture of what it means to do all the work of a normal household.

Personal qualifications are also very important. The home economist in rehabilitation should have a special interest and aptitude for working with handicapped men, women, and children and be able to inspire their confidence. The consultant should be able to work with people of varying educational and social backgrounds. In addition, the consultant should be flexible and imaginative in any approach to homemaking problems.

There are no licensing or certification requirements for this work, but qualified home economists often become members of the American Home Economics Association.

Opportunities

The job outlook for home economists is generally favorable. Population growth is expected to increase the need for home service and international home economists, particularly in family planning programs. In addition, a growing recognition of the work of these professionals in areas such as consumer education, nutrition, family economics, and child care is expected to result in increased demands for services.

Teaching jobs in elementary and secondary schools are limited and there is considerable competition for available openings. However, home economists with advanced degrees should find broader opportunities for teaching at the college or university level.

The advancement of home economists in any organization is dependent on the gaining of relevant work experience and the completion of advanced education programs.

For further information, contact:
American Home Economics Association

HOW TO TAKE A TEST

I. YOU MUST PASS AN EXAMINATION

A. WHAT EVERY CANDIDATE SHOULD KNOW

Examination applicants often ask us for help in preparing for the written test. What can I study in advance? What kinds of questions will be asked? How will the test be given? How will the papers be graded?

As an applicant for a civil service examination, you may be wondering about some of these things. Our purpose here is to suggest effective methods of advance study and to describe civil service examinations.

Your chances for success on this examination can be increased if you know how to prepare. Those "pre-examination jitters" can be reduced if you know what to expect. You can even experience an adventure in good citizenship if you know why civil service exams are given.

B. WHY ARE CIVIL SERVICE EXAMINATIONS GIVEN?

Civil service examinations are important to you in two ways. As a citizen, you want public jobs filled by employees who know how to do their work. As a job seeker, you want a fair chance to compete for that job on an equal footing with other candidates. The best-known means of accomplishing this two-fold goal is the competitive examination.

Exams are widely publicized throughout the nation. They may be administered for jobs in federal, state, city, municipal, town or village governments or agencies.

Any citizen may apply, with some limitations, such as the age or residence of applicants. Your experience and education may be reviewed to see whether you meet the requirements for the particular examination. When these requirements exist, they are reasonable and applied consistently to all applicants. Thus, a competitive examination may cause you some uneasiness now, but it is your privilege and safeguard.

C. HOW ARE CIVIL SERVICE EXAMS DEVELOPED?

Examinations are carefully written by trained technicians who are specialists in the field known as "psychological measurement," in consultation with recognized authorities in the field of work that the test will cover. These experts recommend the subject matter areas or skills to be tested; only those knowledges or skills important to your success on the job are included. The most reliable books and source materials available are used as references. Together, the experts and technicians judge the difficulty level of the questions.

Test technicians know how to phrase questions so that the problem is clearly stated. Their ethics do not permit "trick" or "catch" questions. Questions may have been tried out on sample groups, or subjected to statistical analysis, to determine their usefulness.

Written tests are often used in combination with performance tests, ratings of training and experience, and oral interviews. All of these measures combine to form the best-known means of finding the right person for the right job.

II. HOW TO PASS THE WRITTEN TEST

A. NATURE OF THE EXAMINATION

To prepare intelligently for civil service examinations, you should know how they differ from school examinations you have taken. In school you were assigned certain definite pages to read or subjects to cover. The examination questions were quite detailed and usually emphasized memory. Civil service exams, on the other hand, try to discover your present ability to perform the duties of a position, plus your potentiality to learn these duties. In other words, a civil service exam attempts to predict how successful you will be. Questions cover such a broad area that they cannot be as minute and detailed as school exam questions.

In the public service similar kinds of work, or positions, are grouped together in one "class." This process is known as *position-classification.* All the positions in a class are paid according to the salary range for that class. One class title covers all of these positions, and they are all tested by the same examination.

B. FOUR BASIC STEPS

1) Study the announcement

How, then, can you know what subjects to study? Our best answer is: "Learn as much as possible about the class of positions for which you've applied." The exam will test the knowledge, skills and abilities needed to do the work.

Your most valuable source of information about the position you want is the official exam announcement. This announcement lists the training and experience qualifications. Check these standards and apply only if you come reasonably close to meeting them.

The brief description of the position in the examination announcement offers some clues to the subjects which will be tested. Think about the job itself. Review the duties in your mind. Can you perform them, or are there some in which you are rusty? Fill in the blank spots in your preparation.

Many jurisdictions preview the written test in the exam announcement by including a section called "Knowledge and Abilities Required," "Scope of the Examination," or some similar heading. Here you will find out specifically what fields will be tested.

2) Review your own background

Once you learn in general what the position is all about, and what you need to know to do the work, ask yourself which subjects you already know fairly well and which need improvement. You may wonder whether to concentrate on improving your strong areas or on building some background in your fields of weakness. When the announcement has specified "some knowledge" or "considerable knowledge," or has used adjectives like "beginning principles of..." or "advanced ... methods," you can get a clue as to the number and difficulty of questions to be asked in any given field. More questions, and hence broader coverage, would be included for those subjects which are more important in the work. Now weigh your strengths and weaknesses against the job requirements and prepare accordingly.

3) Determine the level of the position

Another way to tell how intensively you should prepare is to understand the level of the job for which you are applying. Is it the entering level? In other words, is this the position in which beginners in a field of work are hired? Or is it an intermediate or advanced level? Sometimes this is indicated by such words as "Junior" or "Senior" in the class title. Other jurisdictions use Roman numerals to designate the level – Clerk I, Clerk II, for example. The word "Supervisor" sometimes appears in the title. If the level is not indicated by the title, check the description of duties. Will you be working under very close supervision, or will you have responsibility for independent decisions in this work?

4) Choose appropriate study materials

Now that you know the subjects to be examined and the relative amount of each subject to be covered, you can choose suitable study materials. For beginning level jobs, or even advanced ones, if you have a pronounced weakness in some aspect of your training, read a modern, standard textbook in that field. Be sure it is up to date and has general coverage. Such books are normally available at your library, and the librarian will be glad to help you locate one. For entry-level positions, questions of appropriate difficulty are chosen – neither highly advanced questions, nor those too simple. Such questions require careful thought but not advanced training.

If the position for which you are applying is technical or advanced, you will read more advanced, specialized material. If you are already familiar with the basic principles of your field, elementary textbooks would waste your time. Concentrate on advanced textbooks and technical periodicals. Think through the concepts and review difficult problems in your field.

These are all general sources. You can get more ideas on your own initiative, following these leads. For example, training manuals and publications of the government agency which employs workers in your field can be useful, particularly for technical and professional positions. A letter or visit to the government department involved may result in more specific study suggestions, and certainly will provide you with a more definite idea of the exact nature of the position you are seeking.

III. KINDS OF TESTS

Tests are used for purposes other than measuring knowledge and ability to perform specified duties. For some positions, it is equally important to test ability to make adjustments to new situations or to profit from training. In others, basic mental abilities not dependent on information are essential. Questions which test these things may not appear as pertinent to the duties of the position as those which test for knowledge and information. Yet they are often highly important parts of a fair examination. For very general questions, it is almost impossible to help you direct your study efforts. What we can do is to point out some of the more common of these general abilities needed in public service positions and describe some typical questions.

1) General information

Broad, general information has been found useful for predicting job success in some kinds of work. This is tested in a variety of ways, from vocabulary lists to questions about current events. Basic background in some field of work, such as sociology or economics, may be sampled in a group of questions. Often these are principles which have become familiar to most persons through exposure rather than through formal training. It is difficult to advise you how to study for these questions; being alert to the world around you is our best suggestion.

2) Verbal ability

An example of an ability needed in many positions is verbal or language ability. Verbal ability is, in brief, the ability to use and understand words. Vocabulary and grammar tests are typical measures of this ability. Reading comprehension or paragraph interpretation questions are common in many kinds of civil service tests. You are given a paragraph of written material and asked to find its central meaning.

3) Numerical ability

Number skills can be tested by the familiar arithmetic problem, by checking paired lists of numbers to see which are alike and which are different, or by interpreting charts and graphs. In the latter test, a graph may be printed in the test booklet which you are asked to use as the basis for answering questions.

4) Observation

A popular test for law-enforcement positions is the observation test. A picture is shown to you for several minutes, then taken away. Questions about the picture test your ability to observe both details and larger elements.

5) Following directions

In many positions in the public service, the employee must be able to carry out written instructions dependably and accurately. You may be given a chart with several columns, each column listing a variety of information. The questions require you to carry out directions involving the information given in the chart.

6) Skills and aptitudes

Performance tests effectively measure some manual skills and aptitudes. When the skill is one in which you are trained, such as typing or shorthand, you can practice. These tests are often very much like those given in business school or high school courses. For many of the other skills and aptitudes, however, no short-time preparation can be made. Skills and abilities natural to you or that you have developed throughout your lifetime are being tested.

Many of the general questions just described provide all the data needed to answer the questions and ask you to use your reasoning ability to find the answers. Your best preparation for these tests, as well as for tests of facts and ideas, is to be at your physical and mental best. You, no doubt, have your own methods of getting into an exam-taking mood and keeping "in shape." The next section lists some ideas on this subject.

IV. KINDS OF QUESTIONS

Only rarely is the "essay" question, which you answer in narrative form, used in civil service tests. Civil service tests are usually of the short-answer type. Full instructions for answering these questions will be given to you at the examination. But in case this is your first experience with short-answer questions and separate answer sheets, here is what you need to know:

1) Multiple-choice Questions

Most popular of the short-answer questions is the "multiple choice" or "best answer" question. It can be used, for example, to test for factual knowledge, ability to solve problems or judgment in meeting situations found at work.

A multiple-choice question is normally one of three types—

- It can begin with an incomplete statement followed by several possible endings. You are to find the one ending which *best* completes the statement, although some of the others may not be entirely wrong.
- It can also be a complete statement in the form of a question which is answered by choosing one of the statements listed.
- It can be in the form of a problem – again you select the best answer.

Here is an example of a multiple-choice question with a discussion which should give you some clues as to the method for choosing the right answer:

When an employee has a complaint about his assignment, the action which will *best* help him overcome his difficulty is to

- A. discuss his difficulty with his coworkers
- B. take the problem to the head of the organization
- C. take the problem to the person who gave him the assignment
- D. say nothing to anyone about his complaint

In answering this question, you should study each of the choices to find which is best. Consider choice "A" – Certainly an employee may discuss his complaint with fellow employees, but no change or improvement can result, and the complaint remains unresolved. Choice "B" is a poor choice since the head of the organization probably does not know what assignment you have been given, and taking your problem to him is known as "going over the head" of the supervisor. The supervisor, or person who made the assignment, is the person who can clarify it or correct any injustice. Choice "C" is, therefore, correct. To say nothing, as in choice "D," is unwise. Supervisors have and interest in knowing the problems employees are facing, and the employee is seeking a solution to his problem.

2) True/False Questions

The "true/false" or "right/wrong" form of question is sometimes used. Here a complete statement is given. Your job is to decide whether the statement is right or wrong.

SAMPLE: A person-to-person long-distance telephone call costs less than a station-to-station call to the same city.

This statement is wrong, or false, since person-to-person calls are more expensive.

This is not a complete list of all possible question forms, although most of the others are variations of these common types. You will always get complete directions for answering questions. Be sure you understand *how* to mark your answers – ask questions until you do.

V. RECORDING YOUR ANSWERS

For an examination with very few applicants, you may be told to record your answers in the test booklet itself. Separate answer sheets are much more common. If this separate answer sheet is to be scored by machine – and this is often the case – it is highly important that you mark your answers correctly in order to get credit.

An electric scoring machine is often used in civil service offices because of the speed with which papers can be scored. Machine-scored answer sheets must be marked with a pencil, which will be given to you. This pencil has a high graphite content which responds to the electric scoring machine. As a matter of fact, stray dots may register as answers, so do not let your pencil rest on the answer sheet while you are pondering the correct answer. Also, if your pencil lead breaks or is otherwise defective, ask for another.

Since the answer sheet will be dropped in a slot in the scoring machine, be careful not to bend the corners or get the paper crumpled.

The answer sheet normally has five vertical columns of numbers, with 30 numbers to a column. These numbers correspond to the question numbers in your test booklet. After each number, going across the page are four or five pairs of dotted lines. These short dotted lines have small letters or numbers above them. The first two pairs may also have a "T" or "F" above the letters. This indicates that the first two pairs only are to be used if the questions are of the true-false type. If the questions are multiple choice, disregard the "T" and "F" and pay attention only to the small letters or numbers.

Answer your questions in the manner of the sample that follows:

32. The largest city in the United States is
- A. Washington, D.C.
- B. New York City
- C. Chicago
- D. Detroit
- E. San Francisco

1) Choose the answer you think is best. (New York City is the largest, so "B" is correct.)
2) Find the row of dotted lines numbered the same as the question you are answering. (Find row number 32)
3) Find the pair of dotted lines corresponding to the answer. (Find the pair of lines under the mark "B.")
4) Make a solid black mark between the dotted lines.

VI. BEFORE THE TEST

Common sense will help you find procedures to follow to get ready for an examination. Too many of us, however, overlook these sensible measures. Indeed, nervousness and fatigue have been found to be the most serious reasons why applicants fail to do their best on civil service tests. Here is a list of reminders:

- Begin your preparation early – Don't wait until the last minute to go scurrying around for books and materials or to find out what the position is all about.
- Prepare continuously – An hour a night for a week is better than an all-night cram session. This has been definitely established. What is more, a night a

week for a month will return better dividends than crowding your study into a shorter period of time.

- Locate the place of the exam – You have been sent a notice telling you when and where to report for the examination. If the location is in a different town or otherwise unfamiliar to you, it would be well to inquire the best route and learn something about the building.
- Relax the night before the test – Allow your mind to rest. Do not study at all that night. Plan some mild recreation or diversion; then go to bed early and get a good night's sleep.
- Get up early enough to make a leisurely trip to the place for the test – This way unforeseen events, traffic snarls, unfamiliar buildings, etc. will not upset you.
- Dress comfortably – A written test is not a fashion show. You will be known by number and not by name, so wear something comfortable.
- Leave excess paraphernalia at home – Shopping bags and odd bundles will get in your way. You need bring only the items mentioned in the official notice you received; usually everything you need is provided. Do not bring reference books to the exam. They will only confuse those last minutes and be taken away from you when in the test room.
- Arrive somewhat ahead of time – If because of transportation schedules you must get there very early, bring a newspaper or magazine to take your mind off yourself while waiting.
- Locate the examination room – When you have found the proper room, you will be directed to the seat or part of the room where you will sit. Sometimes you are given a sheet of instructions to read while you are waiting. Do not fill out any forms until you are told to do so; just read them and be prepared.
- Relax and prepare to listen to the instructions
- If you have any physical problem that may keep you from doing your best, be sure to tell the test administrator. If you are sick or in poor health, you really cannot do your best on the exam. You can come back and take the test some other time.

VII. AT THE TEST

The day of the test is here and you have the test booklet in your hand. The temptation to get going is very strong. Caution! There is more to success than knowing the right answers. You must know how to identify your papers and understand variations in the type of short-answer question used in this particular examination. Follow these suggestions for maximum results from your efforts:

1) Cooperate with the monitor

The test administrator has a duty to create a situation in which you can be as much at ease as possible. He will give instructions, tell you when to begin, check to see that you are marking your answer sheet correctly, and so on. He is not there to guard you, although he will see that your competitors do not take unfair advantage. He wants to help you do your best.

2) Listen to all instructions

Don't jump the gun! Wait until you understand all directions. In most civil service tests you get more time than you need to answer the questions. So don't be in a hurry.

Read each word of instructions until you clearly understand the meaning. Study the examples, listen to all announcements and follow directions. Ask questions if you do not understand what to do.

3) Identify your papers

Civil service exams are usually identified by number only. You will be assigned a number; you must not put your name on your test papers. Be sure to copy your number correctly. Since more than one exam may be given, copy your exact examination title.

4) Plan your time

Unless you are told that a test is a "speed" or "rate of work" test, speed itself is usually not important. Time enough to answer all the questions will be provided, but this does not mean that you have all day. An overall time limit has been set. Divide the total time (in minutes) by the number of questions to determine the approximate time you have for each question.

5) Do not linger over difficult questions

If you come across a difficult question, mark it with a paper clip (useful to have along) and come back to it when you have been through the booklet. One caution if you do this – be sure to skip a number on your answer sheet as well. Check often to be sure that you have not lost your place and that you are marking in the row numbered the same as the question you are answering.

6) Read the questions

Be sure you know what the question asks! Many capable people are unsuccessful because they failed to *read* the questions correctly.

7) Answer all questions

Unless you have been instructed that a penalty will be deducted for incorrect answers, it is better to guess than to omit a question.

8) Speed tests

It is often better NOT to guess on speed tests. It has been found that on timed tests people are tempted to spend the last few seconds before time is called in marking answers at random – without even reading them – in the hope of picking up a few extra points. To discourage this practice, the instructions may warn you that your score will be "corrected" for guessing. That is, a penalty will be applied. The incorrect answers will be deducted from the correct ones, or some other penalty formula will be used.

9) Review your answers

If you finish before time is called, go back to the questions you guessed or omitted to give them further thought. Review other answers if you have time.

10) Return your test materials

If you are ready to leave before others have finished or time is called, take ALL your materials to the monitor and leave quietly. Never take any test material with you. The monitor can discover whose papers are not complete, and taking a test booklet may be grounds for disqualification.

VIII. EXAMINATION TECHNIQUES

1) Read the general instructions carefully. These are usually printed on the first page of the exam booklet. As a rule, these instructions refer to the timing of the examination; the fact that you should not start work until the signal and must stop work at a signal, etc. If there are any *special* instructions, such as a choice of questions to be answered, make sure that you note this instruction carefully.

2) When you are ready to start work on the examination, that is as soon as the signal has been given, read the instructions to each question booklet, underline any key words or phrases, such as *least, best, outline, describe* and the like. In this way you will tend to answer as requested rather than discover on reviewing your paper that you *listed without describing*, that you selected the *worst* choice rather than the *best* choice, etc.

3) If the examination is of the objective or multiple-choice type – that is, each question will also give a series of possible answers: A, B, C or D, and you are called upon to select the best answer and write the letter next to that answer on your answer paper – it is advisable to start answering each question in turn. There may be anywhere from 50 to 100 such questions in the three or four hours allotted and you can see how much time would be taken if you read through all the questions before beginning to answer any. Furthermore, if you come across a question or group of questions which you know would be difficult to answer, it would undoubtedly affect your handling of all the other questions.

4) If the examination is of the essay type and contains but a few questions, it is a moot point as to whether you should read all the questions before starting to answer any one. Of course, if you are given a choice – say five out of seven and the like – then it is essential to read all the questions so you can eliminate the two that are most difficult. If, however, you are asked to answer all the questions, there may be danger in trying to answer the easiest one first because you may find that you will spend too much time on it. The best technique is to answer the first question, then proceed to the second, etc.

5) Time your answers. Before the exam begins, write down the time it started, then add the time allowed for the examination and write down the time it must be completed, then divide the time available somewhat as follows:
   - If 3-1/2 hours are allowed, that would be 210 minutes. If you have 80 objective-type questions, that would be an average of 2-1/2 minutes per question. Allow yourself no more than 2 minutes per question, or a total of 160 minutes, which will permit about 50 minutes to review.
   - If for the time allotment of 210 minutes there are 7 essay questions to answer, that would average about 30 minutes a question. Give yourself only 25 minutes per question so that you have about 35 minutes to review.

6) The most important instruction is to *read each question* and make sure you know what is wanted. The second most important instruction is to *time yourself properly* so that you answer every question. The third most

important instruction is to *answer every question.* Guess if you have to but include something for each question. Remember that you will receive no credit for a blank and will probably receive some credit if you write something in answer to an essay question. If you guess a letter – say "B" for a multiple-choice question – you may have guessed right. If you leave a blank as an answer to a multiple-choice question, the examiners may respect your feelings but it will not add a point to your score. Some exams may penalize you for wrong answers, so in such cases *only,* you may not want to guess unless you have some basis for your answer.

7) Suggestions
   a. Objective-type questions
      1. Examine the question booklet for proper sequence of pages and questions
      2. Read all instructions carefully
      3. Skip any question which seems too difficult; return to it after all other questions have been answered
      4. Apportion your time properly; do not spend too much time on any single question or group of questions
      5. Note and underline key words – *all, most, fewest, least, best, worst, same, opposite,* etc.
      6. Pay particular attention to negatives
      7. Note unusual option, e.g., unduly long, short, complex, different or similar in content to the body of the question
      8. Observe the use of "hedging" words – *probably, may, most likely,* etc.
      9. Make sure that your answer is put next to the same number as the question
      10. Do not second-guess unless you have good reason to believe the second answer is definitely more correct
      11. Cross out original answer if you decide another answer is more accurate; do not erase until you are ready to hand your paper in
      12. Answer all questions; guess unless instructed otherwise
      13. Leave time for review

   b. Essay questions
      1. Read each question carefully
      2. Determine exactly what is wanted. Underline key words or phrases.
      3. Decide on outline or paragraph answer
      4. Include many different points and elements unless asked to develop any one or two points or elements
      5. Show impartiality by giving pros and cons unless directed to select one side only
      6. Make and write down any assumptions you find necessary to answer the questions
      7. Watch your English, grammar, punctuation and choice of words
      8. Time your answers; don't crowd material

8) Answering the essay question

Most essay questions can be answered by framing the specific response around several key words or ideas. Here are a few such key words or ideas:

M's: manpower, materials, methods, money, management
P's: purpose, program, policy, plan, procedure, practice, problems, pitfalls, personnel, public relations

a. Six basic steps in handling problems:
   1. Preliminary plan and background development
   2. Collect information, data and facts
   3. Analyze and interpret information, data and facts
   4. Analyze and develop solutions as well as make recommendations
   5. Prepare report and sell recommendations
   6. Install recommendations and follow up effectiveness

b. Pitfalls to avoid
   1. *Taking things for granted* – A statement of the situation does not necessarily imply that each of the elements is necessarily true; for example, a complaint may be invalid and biased so that all that can be taken for granted is that a complaint has been registered
   2. *Considering only one side of a situation* – Wherever possible, indicate several alternatives and then point out the reasons you selected the best one
   3. *Failing to indicate follow up* – Whenever your answer indicates action on your part, make certain that you will take proper follow-up action to see how successful your recommendations, procedures or actions turn out to be
   4. *Taking too long in answering any single question* – Remember to time your answers properly

IX. AFTER THE TEST

Scoring procedures differ in detail among civil service jurisdictions although the general principles are the same. Whether the papers are hand-scored or graded by machine we have described, they are nearly always graded by number. That is, the person who marks the paper knows only the number – never the name – of the applicant. Not until all the papers have been graded will they be matched with names. If other tests, such as training and experience or oral interview ratings have been given, scores will be combined. Different parts of the examination usually have different weights. For example, the written test might count 60 percent of the final grade, and a rating of training and experience 40 percent. In many jurisdictions, veterans will have a certain number of points added to their grades.

After the final grade has been determined, the names are placed in grade order and an eligible list is established. There are various methods for resolving ties between those who get the same final grade – probably the most common is to place first the name of the person whose application was received first. Job offers are made from the eligible list in the order the names appear on it. You will be notified of your grade and your rank as soon as all these computations have been made. This will be done as rapidly as possible.

People who are found to meet the requirements in the announcement are called "eligibles." Their names are put on a list of eligible candidates. An eligible's chances of getting a job depend on how high he stands on this list and how fast agencies are filling jobs from the list.

When a job is to be filled from a list of eligibles, the agency asks for the names of people on the list of eligibles for that job. When the civil service commission receives this request, it sends to the agency the names of the three people highest on this list. Or, if the job to be filled has specialized requirements, the office sends the agency the names of the top three persons who meet these requirements from the general list.

The appointing officer makes a choice from among the three people whose names were sent to him. If the selected person accepts the appointment, the names of the others are put back on the list to be considered for future openings.

That is the rule in hiring from all kinds of eligible lists, whether they are for typist, carpenter, chemist, or something else. For every vacancy, the appointing officer has his choice of any one of the top three eligibles on the list. This explains why the person whose name is on top of the list sometimes does not get an appointment when some of the persons lower on the list do. If the appointing officer chooses the second or third eligible, the No. 1 eligible does not get a job at once, but stays on the list until he is appointed or the list is terminated.

X. HOW TO PASS THE INTERVIEW TEST

The examination for which you applied requires an oral interview test. You have already taken the written test and you are now being called for the interview test – the final part of the formal examination.

You may think that it is not possible to prepare for an interview test and that there are no procedures to follow during an interview. Our purpose is to point out some things you can do in advance that will help you and some good rules to follow and pitfalls to avoid while you are being interviewed.

What is an interview supposed to test?

The written examination is designed to test the technical knowledge and competence of the candidate; the oral is designed to evaluate intangible qualities, not readily measured otherwise, and to establish a list showing the relative fitness of each candidate – as measured against his competitors – for the position sought. Scoring is not on the basis of "right" and "wrong," but on a sliding scale of values ranging from "not passable" to "outstanding." As a matter of fact, it is possible to achieve a relatively low score without a single "incorrect" answer because of evident weakness in the qualities being measured.

Occasionally, an examination may consist entirely of an oral test – either an individual or a group oral. In such cases, information is sought concerning the technical knowledges and abilities of the candidate, since there has been no written examination for this purpose. More commonly, however, an oral test is used to supplement a written examination.

Who conducts interviews?

The composition of oral boards varies among different jurisdictions. In nearly all, a representative of the personnel department serves as chairman. One of the members of the board may be a representative of the department in which the candidate would work. In some cases, "outside experts" are used, and, frequently, a businessman or some other representative of the general public is asked to serve. Labor and management or other special groups may be represented. The aim is to secure the services of experts in the appropriate field.

However the board is composed, it is a good idea (and not at all improper or unethical) to ascertain in advance of the interview who the members are and what groups they represent. When you are introduced to them, you will have some idea of their backgrounds and interests, and at least you will not stutter and stammer over their names.

What should be done before the interview?

While knowledge about the board members is useful and takes some of the surprise element out of the interview, there is other preparation which is more substantive. It *is* possible to prepare for an oral interview – in several ways:

1) Keep a copy of your application and review it carefully before the interview

This may be the only document before the oral board, and the starting point of the interview. Know what education and experience you have listed there, and the sequence and dates of all of it. Sometimes the board will ask you to review the highlights of your experience for them; you should not have to hem and haw doing it.

2) Study the class specification and the examination announcement

Usually, the oral board has one or both of these to guide them. The qualities, characteristics or knowledges required by the position sought are stated in these documents. They offer valuable clues as to the nature of the oral interview. For example, if the job involves supervisory responsibilities, the announcement will usually indicate that knowledge of modern supervisory methods and the qualifications of the candidate as a supervisor will be tested. If so, you can expect such questions, frequently in the form of a hypothetical situation which you are expected to solve. NEVER go into an oral without knowledge of the duties and responsibilities of the job you seek.

3) Think through each qualification required

Try to visualize the kind of questions you would ask if you were a board member. How well could you answer them? Try especially to appraise your own knowledge and background in each area, *measured against the job sought*, and identify any areas in which you are weak. Be critical and realistic – do not flatter yourself.

4) Do some general reading in areas in which you feel you may be weak

For example, if the job involves supervision and your past experience has NOT, some general reading in supervisory methods and practices, particularly in the field of human relations, might be useful. Do NOT study agency procedures or detailed manuals. The oral board will be testing your understanding and capacity, not your memory.

5) Get a good night's sleep and watch your general health and mental attitude

You will want a clear head at the interview. Take care of a cold or any other minor ailment, and of course, no hangovers.

What should be done on the day of the interview?

Now comes the day of the interview itself. Give yourself plenty of time to get there. Plan to arrive somewhat ahead of the scheduled time, particularly if your appointment is in the fore part of the day. If a previous candidate fails to appear, the board might be ready for you a bit early. By early afternoon an oral board is almost invariably behind schedule if there are many candidates, and you may have to wait.

Take along a book or magazine to read, or your application to review, but leave any extraneous material in the waiting room when you go in for your interview. In any event, relax and compose yourself.

The matter of dress is important. The board is forming impressions about you – from your experience, your manners, your attitude, and your appearance. Give your personal appearance careful attention. Dress your best, but not your flashiest. Choose conservative, appropriate clothing, and be sure it is immaculate. This is a business interview, and your appearance should indicate that you regard it as such. Besides, being well groomed and properly dressed will help boost your confidence.

Sooner or later, someone will call your name and escort you into the interview room. *This is it.* From here on you are on your own. It is too late for any more preparation. But remember, you asked for this opportunity to prove your fitness, and you are here because your request was granted.

What happens when you go in?

The usual sequence of events will be as follows: The clerk (who is often the board stenographer) will introduce you to the chairman of the oral board, who will introduce you to the other members of the board. Acknowledge the introductions before you sit down. Do not be surprised if you find a microphone facing you or a stenotypist sitting by. Oral interviews are usually recorded in the event of an appeal or other review.

Usually the chairman of the board will open the interview by reviewing the highlights of your education and work experience from your application – primarily for the benefit of the other members of the board, as well as to get the material into the record. Do not interrupt or comment unless there is an error or significant misinterpretation; if that is the case, do not hesitate. But do not quibble about insignificant matters. Also, he will usually ask you some question about your education, experience or your present job – partly to get you to start talking and to establish the interviewing "rapport." He may start the actual questioning, or turn it over to one of the other members. Frequently, each member undertakes the questioning on a particular area, one in which he is perhaps most competent, so you can expect each member to participate in the examination. Because time is limited, you may also expect some rather abrupt switches in the direction the questioning takes, so do not be upset by it. Normally, a board member will not pursue a single line of questioning unless he discovers a particular strength or weakness.

After each member has participated, the chairman will usually ask whether any member has any further questions, then will ask you if you have anything you wish to add. Unless you are expecting this question, it may floor you. Worse, it may start you off on an extended, extemporaneous speech. The board is not usually seeking more information. The question is principally to offer you a last opportunity to present further qualifications or to indicate that you have nothing to add. So, if you feel that a significant qualification or characteristic has been overlooked, it is proper to point it out in a sentence or so. Do not compliment the board on the thoroughness of their examination – they have been sketchy, and you know it. If you wish, merely say, "No thank you, I have nothing further to add." This is a point where you can "talk yourself out" of a good impression or fail to present an important bit of information. Remember, *you close the interview yourself.*

The chairman will then say, "That is all, Mr. _____, thank you." Do not be startled; the interview is over, and quicker than you think. Thank him, gather your belongings and take your leave. Save your sigh of relief for the other side of the door.

How to put your best foot forward

Throughout this entire process, you may feel that the board individually and collectively is trying to pierce your defenses, seek out your hidden weaknesses and embarrass and confuse you. Actually, this is not true. They are obliged to make an appraisal of your qualifications for the job you are seeking, and they want to see you in your best light. Remember, they must interview all candidates and a non-cooperative candidate may become a failure in spite of their best efforts to bring out his qualifications. Here are 15 suggestions that will help you:

1) Be natural – Keep your attitude confident, not cocky

If you are not confident that you can do the job, do not expect the board to be. Do not apologize for your weaknesses, try to bring out your strong points. The board is interested in a positive, not negative, presentation. Cockiness will antagonize any board member and make him wonder if you are covering up a weakness by a false show of strength.

2) Get comfortable, but don't lounge or sprawl

Sit erectly but not stiffly. A careless posture may lead the board to conclude that you are careless in other things, or at least that you are not impressed by the importance of the occasion. Either conclusion is natural, even if incorrect. Do not fuss with your clothing, a pencil or an ashtray. Your hands may occasionally be useful to emphasize a point; do not let them become a point of distraction.

3) Do not wisecrack or make small talk

This is a serious situation, and your attitude should show that you consider it as such. Further, the time of the board is limited – they do not want to waste it, and neither should you.

4) Do not exaggerate your experience or abilities

In the first place, from information in the application or other interviews and sources, the board may know more about you than you think. Secondly, you probably will not get away with it. An experienced board is rather adept at spotting such a situation, so do not take the chance.

5) If you know a board member, do not make a point of it, yet do not hide it

Certainly you are not fooling him, and probably not the other members of the board. Do not try to take advantage of your acquaintanceship – it will probably do you little good.

6) Do not dominate the interview

Let the board do that. They will give you the clues – do not assume that you have to do all the talking. Realize that the board has a number of questions to ask you, and do not try to take up all the interview time by showing off your extensive knowledge of the answer to the first one.

7) Be attentive

You only have 20 minutes or so, and you should keep your attention at its sharpest throughout. When a member is addressing a problem or question to you, give him your undivided attention. Address your reply principally to him, but do not exclude the other board members.

8) Do not interrupt

A board member may be stating a problem for you to analyze. He will ask you a question when the time comes. Let him state the problem, and wait for the question.

9) Make sure you understand the question

Do not try to answer until you are sure what the question is. If it is not clear, restate it in your own words or ask the board member to clarify it for you. However, do not haggle about minor elements.

10) Reply promptly but not hastily

A common entry on oral board rating sheets is "candidate responded readily," or "candidate hesitated in replies." Respond as promptly and quickly as you can, but do not jump to a hasty, ill-considered answer.

11) Do not be peremptory in your answers

A brief answer is proper – but do not fire your answer back. That is a losing game from your point of view. The board member can probably ask questions much faster than you can answer them.

12) Do not try to create the answer you think the board member wants

He is interested in what kind of mind you have and how it works – not in playing games. Furthermore, he can usually spot this practice and will actually grade you down on it.

13) Do not switch sides in your reply merely to agree with a board member

Frequently, a member will take a contrary position merely to draw you out and to see if you are willing and able to defend your point of view. Do not start a debate, yet do not surrender a good position. If a position is worth taking, it is worth defending.

14) Do not be afraid to admit an error in judgment if you are shown to be wrong

The board knows that you are forced to reply without any opportunity for careful consideration. Your answer may be demonstrably wrong. If so, admit it and get on with the interview.

15) Do not dwell at length on your present job

The opening question may relate to your present assignment. Answer the question but do not go into an extended discussion. You are being examined for a *new* job, not your present one. As a matter of fact, try to phrase ALL your answers in terms of the job for which you are being examined.

Basis of Rating

Probably you will forget most of these "do's" and "don'ts" when you walk into the oral interview room. Even remembering them all will not ensure you a passing grade. Perhaps you did not have the qualifications in the first place. But remembering them will help you to put your best foot forward, without treading on the toes of the board members.

Rumor and popular opinion to the contrary notwithstanding, an oral board wants you to make the best appearance possible. They know you are under pressure – but they also want to see how you respond to it as a guide to what your reaction would be under the pressures of the job you seek. They will be influenced by the degree of poise you display, the personal traits you show and the manner in which you respond.

EXAMINATION SECTION

EXAMINATION SECTION TEST 1

DIRECTIONS: Each question or incomplete statement is followed by several suggested answers or completions. Select the one that BEST answers the question or completes the statement. *PRINT THE LETTER OF THE CORRECT ANSWER IN THE SPACE AT THE RIGHT.*

1. Of the following, the requisition which is CORRECT for the number of servings indicated is

   A. 300 lbs. eviscerated frozen turkey for 480 servings
   B. 190 lbs. cured ham, bone in, for ham steaks for 600 servilngs
   C. 100 lbs. whole beef liver for 520 servings
   D. 380 lbs. veal leg, bone in, for roast veal for 500 servings

2. Of the following, the LEAST effective way of effecting portion control is by means of

   A. instruction of personnel responsible for serving food
   B. purchase of pre-portioned foods
   C. use of standardized serving utensils
   D. preparation and use of standardized recipes

3. The MOST important reason for using a manual in a dietary department is that it serves as a

   A. means of preventing duplication of work
   B. tool for achieving orderly operations
   C. system for controlling food waste
   D. system for controlling food costs

4. Of the following, the MOST important reason for using standardized recipes is that they provide

   A. uniformity of quality and quantity of the product
   B. greater control of raw food costs
   C. saving of labor hours resulting in lower cost
   D. guidance in pre-planning of menus

5. From the standpoint of the dietitian, the CHIEF advantage of centralized as compared to decentralized food service is that

   A. space needed for floor pantries in a decentralized service can be used instead for other purposes
   B. better controls can be exercised by the dietitian
   C. less service is required from the nursing department
   D. it eliminates complaints that pantry noises on the floor disturb the patients

6. Assume that the dishwashing load is unusually heavy for the facilities provided. Of the following, the MOST expedient method for reducing the load would be to

   A. stagger the meal hours
   B. use paper cups for beverages

C. increase the number of employees handling the operation
D. decrease the timing on the machine wash and rinse operations

7. The amount of freezer space necessary in a kitchen will depend MAINLY upon the

A. frequency of delivery service
B. amount of money that can be tied up in stored items
C. number of frozen foods used on the menu
D. savings effected in purchasing in bulk at advantageous times

8. Before recommending a time-saving device, the MOST important factor to be considered is

A. whether it will be used frequently
B. the amount of maintenance which will be required
C. the number of productive labor hours which will be saved
D. the space it will require

9. Before planning a kitchen layout, it is MOST important to know

A. how much money will be available
B. the relation of the kitchen to other areas
C. the numbers and availability of personnel
D. what types of menus and service will be used

10. Kitchen equipment should be placed PRIMARILY to

A. provide neat, uncluttered appearance
B. avoid cross traffic
C. permit easy access to the main delivery area
D. establish a separate work area for each cook

11. The MAIN advantage of using standardized pans is that

A. the same pan can be used for cooking, serving, and storing
B. fewer pans are required
C. they stack better and require less storage space
D. less time is used to select the right pan for the job

12. Specific cleaning agents and detergents have been recommended for use on various surface materials in order to do a thorough job of cleaning and to maintain the attractive appearance of the material.
Of the following, the one which you would recommend for the purpose indicated is

A. tri-sodium phosphate for cleaning aluminum pots and pans
B. a scouring cleanser with a high percent of abrasive material for cleaning stainless steel tables and trucks
C. a lye base liquid soap for use in automatic dishwashing machines
D. a non-oil base detergent for floors covered with light-colored rubber tile

13. Scraping and prerinsing of dishes before running them through the dishwashing machine is necessary to

A. shorten the time of the washing process
B. reduce the amount of detergent needed
C. prevent blocking of the nozzles in the rinse arm of the machine
D. remove food particles which harden at the wash temperature

14. When purchasing food, the one of the following which should be the deciding factor for determining what is the MOST economical buy is the

A. unit price as purchased
B. cost of edible portion
C. cost of product as served
D. preparation costs

15. When ordering perishable foods, the specification should designate the condition of the foods as of the time of

A. delivery   B. shipment   C. packaging   D. bidding

16. Of the following forms in which meat can be purchased, the form which makes possible MOST accurate portion control is

A. quarters   B. prefabricated
C. carcass   D. wholesale cuts

17. Fresh fruits are generally at their best during certain periods. Of the following, the statement which is LEAST accurate is that

A. cherries are best in June and July
B. cranberries are best from April to September
C. grapefruit is best from November to February
D. California grapes are best from November to February

18. When labor is the MOST important consideration, it is BEST to purchase potatoes

A. whole, unpeeled   B. whole, peeled
C. instant, powdered   D. canned

19. When purchasing grapefruit for an institution, it is BEST to purchase by the

A. pound   B. dozen   C. bushel   D. crate count

20. Of the following, the specification which is LEAST desirable when purchasing fresh vegetables is

A. cauliflower, leaves trimmed to within 1" to 2" from head
B. beets, stems completely removed
C. carrots, topped, tops cut back to less than 1"
D. celery, stalk length 16" and well trimmed

21. When accepting a delivery of a large order of frozen foods, it is MOST important to

A. be sure that the grade which was ordered is received
B. see that the labels are intact
C. check for evidence of defrosting
D. weigh the merchandise to be sure of correct weight

4 (#1)

22. For proper storage of dry and canned food supplies, it is NOT advisable to

    A. place all shelving and stacks close against the wall to prevent falling
    B. stack like items together to facilitate issuing and taking of inventories
    C. store canned goods on shelves or on platforms 4 to 6" off the floor
    D. stack the most recent receipts in back or on the bottom to make the *first in, first out* rule easy to follow

23. If a high bacteria count on the dishes is found in one of the serving units, it is LEAST important to

    A. check the wash and rinse temperature of the dishwashing machine
    B. check the technique for scraping, prerinsing, washing, and rinsing dishes
    C. inspect the serving unit, including all equipment, for cleanliness
    D. arrange for a physical examination of every employee in the department

24. Rodent control is of prime importance in maintaining sanitary conditions. The MOST effective way to eliminate rodents is by

    A. providing regular visits of licensed exterminators
    B. use of traps baited with food
    C. cautious use of rat poisons
    D. elimination of harborages

25. The recommended daily dietary allowance of protein for an aged man is MOST NEARLY _____ gm. per kg. body weight.

    A. .5   B. 1   C. 1.5   D. 2

KEY (CORRECT ANSWERS)

1.	A	11.	A
2.	A	12.	D
3.	B	13.	D
4.	A	14.	C
5.	B	15.	A
6.	B	16.	B
7.	A	17.	B
8.	C	18.	C
9.	D	19.	D
10.	B	20.	B

21.	C
22.	A
23.	D
24.	D
25.	B

TEST 2

DIRECTIONS: Each question or incomplete statement is followed by several suggested answers or completions. Select the one that BEST answers the question or completes the statement. *PRINT THE LETTER OF THE CORRECT ANSWER IN THE SPACE AT THE RIGHT.*

1. The GREATEST amount of protein per unit of body weight is needed during

   A. childhood   B. infancy   C. adolescence   D. pregnancy

2. The thiamine needs of the individual are dependent upon the

   A. total caloric intake   B. body weight
   C. body height   D. age

3. Of the following foods, the BEST source of riboflavin is

   A. lean meat   B. egg   C. milk   D. orange

4. Of the following groups of foods, the one which contains the LARGEST number of alkaline-ash foods is

   A. milk, sugar, and starch
   B. milk, meat, and potatoes
   C. all fruits and vegetables
   D. most fruits, most vegetables, and milk

5. Of the following nutrients, the one which may reduce the amount of radioactive strontium 90 which may be deposited in the body is

   A. vitamin D   B. calcium
   C. oleic acid   D. ascorbic acid

6. If taken in massive doses over a period of time, the vitamin which may cause toxic effects is

   A. ascorbic acid   B. pantothenic acid
   C. vitamin B_{12} D. vitamin A

7. The vitamin which contains cobalt is

   A. vitamin B_{12} B. folic acid
   C. ascorbic acid   D. riboflavin

8. The term *niacin equivalents* refers to

   A. foods which have an equivalent niacin content
   B. the increase necessary when metabolism is accelerated
   C. the quantitative tryptophan-niacin relationship
   D. the minimum amount of niacin which will protect against symptoms of pellagra

9. The blood cholesterol level is MOST affected by

   A. body cholesterol synthesis   B. ingestion of egg yolks
   C. total dietary cholesterol intake D. total fat intake

2 (#2)

10. The calcium is unavailable because it forms an insoluble salt in combination with oxalic acid in

    A. collards   B. carrots   C. beets   D. spinach

11. Following convalescence from gastric surgery, a relatively high proportion of patients experience distressing symptoms after eating.
The diet prescription for this condition is USUALLY

    A. high protein, high fat, low carbohydrate
    B. high protein, low fat, low carbohydrate
    C. high protein, high carbohydrate, low fat
    D. low protein, low fat, high carbohydrate

12. An increase of high residue foods in the diet is indicated in cases of

    A. spastic constipation   B. ulcerative colitis
    C. atonic constipation   D. diverticulitis

13. The dietary treatment for diseases of the liver consists of

    A. high protein, high carbohydrate, and moderate fat intake
    B. moderate protein, low carbohydrate, and low fat intake
    C. high protein, moderate carbohydrate, and moderate fat intake
    D. moderate protein, high carbohydrate, and low fat intake

14. The diet USUALLY prescribed for persons with hyperchlorhydria is _____ diet.

    A. 100 mg. sodium   B. low residue
    C. low phosphorus   D. low purine

15. In the treatment of phenylketonuria, the diet MUST be modified so that

    A. all protein is eliminated from the diet
    B. phenylalanine is completely eliminated from the diet until the child is 5 years old
    C. the serum level of phenylalanine is maintained within normal limits
    D. milk and milk products are the only foods eliminated from the diet

16. When signs of impending hepatic coma appear in a patient with advanced cirrhosis, the diet MOST likely to be ordered is

    A. low protein   B. low carbohydrate
    C. low caloric   D. fat free

17. The one of the following menus which would be BEST to serve to an ulcer patient who follows kosher food laws is

    A. cream of pea soup, cream cheese sandwich, asparagus tips, custard, milk
    B. cream of pea soup, chicken, mashed potatoes, diced carrots, canned pears, milk
    C. tomato juice, beef pattie, baked potato with butter, peas, junket, milk
    D. apple juice, creamed diced shrimp on rice, peas, canned peaches, milk

3 (#2)

18. In the treatment of gout, the one of the following which MUST often be restricted because it may inhibit the excretion of uric acid is

A. carbohydrate B. fats
C. fluids D. calcium

18._____

19. Of the following groups of foods, the one which may be indicated in a gluten-free diet is

A. rye, barley, and macaroni
B. crackers, spaghetti, and rice
C. cream of wheat, cornstarch, and oats
D. corn, potato, and rice

19._____

20. The one of the following which would NOT alleviate the symptoms of the dumping syndrome is

A. small frequent feedings instead of large meals
B. dry meals with fluids taken only between meals
C. emphasis on concentrated forms of carbohydrates
D. avoidance of chilled foods

20._____

21. The one of the following symptoms which is MOST indicative of riboflavin deficiency is

A. poor wound healing
B. fissures at the corners of the mouth
C. bone deformities
D. simple goiter

21._____

22. A preschool child who is allowed to drink as much as 2 quarts of milk daily to the exclusion of adequate amounts of solid foods is MOST likely to be deficient in

A. protein B. riboflavin C. iron D. vitamin A

22._____

23. The ketosis which occurs in uncontrolled diabetes is caused by the excessive oxidation of

A. B-complex vitamins B. fats
C. carbohydrates D. ascorbic acid

23._____

24. *Hidden hunger* may be the result of a diet lacking in sufficient amounts of

A. foods high in cellulose B. high calorie foods
C. protein foods D. protective foods

24._____

25. A possible result of protein deficiency is

A. edema B. heart disease
C. gout D. sprue

25._____

4 (#2)

KEY (CORRECT ANSWERS)

1.	B		11.	A
2.	A		12.	C
3.	C		13.	A
4.	D		14.	B
5.	B		15.	C
6.	D		16.	A
7.	A		17.	A
8.	C		18.	B
9.	A		19.	D
10.	D		20.	C

21. B
22. C
23. B
24. D
25. A

TEST 3

DIRECTIONS: Each question or incomplete statement is followed by several suggested answers or completions. Select the one that BEST answers the question or completes the statement. *PRINT THE LETTER OF THE CORRECT ANSWER IN THE SPACE AT THE RIGHT.*

1. A negative nitrogen balance occurs when

   A. more nitrogen is being ingested than is excreted in the urine
   B. new tissue is being built in periods of rapid growth
   C. dietary protein intake is adequate for tissue synthesis
   D. the body's energy needs must be met from the body's stores of fat and the reserves of protein

2. When planning a diet for an overweight adolescent girl, it is MOST important to consider that

   A. the chief problem is controlling the intake of candy and rich desserts
   B. overweight often disappears by the end of the adolescent period
   C. most problems of overweight are glandular in origin
   D. emotional and social problems are often related to the obesity

3. If a patient with a long-term illness has anorexia, it is MOST important that

   A. he lie down for a half hour before each meal
   B. he be served his favorite foods first
   C. his nutritional requirements be met in spite of his lack of appetite
   D. he be allowed an alcoholic beverage as an appetite stimulant

4. Assume that the bakers have been scheduled to be off duty on Saturday and Sunday. Under these circumstances, the MOST suitable one of the following combinations of desserts for Sunday is

   A. brownie a la mode for dinner; cheesecake (frozen) for supper
   B. apple pie a la mode for dinner; baked bread pudding for supper
   C. butterscotch pie for dinner; canned fruit cocktail with cookies for supper
   D. cherry jello with sliced bananas for dinner; Napoleons for supper

5. To increase consumer satisfaction, it is recommended that whenever possible a choice of menu items be offered.
Of the following, the choice of menu items which is LEAST appropriate for use in a hospital cafeteria is

   A. stewed prunes or fresh frozen orange juice
   B. half grapefruit or canned applesauce
   C. sliced bananas or baked applies
   D. pineapple juice or grapefruit sections

6. When preparing the menu, it is important to consider ease in serving, overall economy, and utilization of manpower and supplies. Of the following menu items, the combination which is LEAST appropriate for a hospital menu is

   A. sliced tomato salad or head lettuce salad
   B. carrot and raisin salad or Waldorf salad
   C. coleslaw or celery and carrot sticks
   D. marinated sliced cucumbers or tossed salad greens

7. Of the following, the one which BEST illustrates the principles of good menu planning is

   A. beef stew, creamed diced potatoes, mixed vegetable salad, bread, butter, chilled fruit cup, coffee, tea or milk
   B. baked stuffed pork chop, mashed potatoes, buttered broccoli, spiced applesauce, bread, butter, raspberry sherbet with vanilla cookies, coffee, tea or milk
   C. French fried shrimp, baked potato, fried eggplant, lettuce salad with Thousand Islands dressing, bread, butter, sugared doughnuts, coffee, tea or milk
   D. cream of celery soup, baked filet of sole, steamed diced potatoes, buttered cauliflower, bread, butter, lemon sherbet, coffee, tea or milk

8. Assume that a disaster has occurred and you have no gas or electricity in your hospital but you have steam and hot water. The feeding census has doubled to 3000. The BEST of the following menus to serve under these circumstances is:

   A. steamed frankfurters, Creole lima beans, pickle slices, bread or rolls, butter, mustard, sliced pineapple, boxed cookies, coffee and milk
   B. cold cuts, potato salad, sliced tomatoes, bread, butter, mustard, fresh apples, coffee, milk
   C. tomato juice, hamburgers on a bun, sliced onion, coleslaw, potato chips, canned applesauce, coffee, milk
   D. egg salad on lettuce, baked potato, bread, butter, hot cocoa, canned fruit cocktail

9. The timing of the cooking of fresh and frozen vegetables must be carefully planned into each day's operation if the final product is to be of top quality when it is served. When cooking vegetables in a steam kettle, the vegetables are added after the water comes to a boil and timing begins when the water reboils. Of the following, the one which would NOT result in a top quality product is cooking of twenty pounds of

   A. fresh broccoli for 15 to 20 minutes
   B. frozen peas for 25 to 30 minutes
   C. fresh asparagus for 5 to 10 minutes
   D. frozen chopped spinach for 10 to 15 minutes

10. Advance preparation enables the dietary department to serve a variety of menu items not otherwise possible. The one of the following items which may be prepared 12 to 24 hours in advance without loss in quality is

   A. Brown Betty
   C. potato salad
   B. stuffed pork chops
   D. spiced pears

11. When the butcher is instructed to process meat for beef stew, he should be instructed to use beef _____ and beef _____.

A. chuck; neck
C. round; ribs

B. loin; chuck
D. neck; loin

11._____

12. Of the following, the food items which are NOT interchangeable in recipes are

12._____

A. chocolate with cocoa and fat
B. fresh whole milk with non-fat dry milk solids and fat plus water
C. baking powder with buttermilk and soda
D. hard flour with soft flour and cornstarch

13. To produce the BEST medium white sauce, you should add for each cup of milk _____ of flour.

13._____

A. 1 teaspoon
C. 1/4 cup

B. 2 tablespoons
D. 8 tablespoons

14. The quality of food when served is greatly affected by the timing of preparation and cooking.
The one of the following which is MOST likely to be of acceptable quality when served is

14._____

A. corn on the cob husked in the morning, refrigerated in plastic bags until 3:30, and cooked for 25 minutes at 4 P.M. for evening meal hour 4:30 to 6 P.M.
B. hamburgers made from beef freshly ground at 7 A.M., seasoned, shaped and panned at 9 A.M., cooked in oven at 10:30 A.M., and distributed to all dining rooms at 11:30 for noon service until 1 P.M.
C. baked potatoes, sorted and washed the day before, panned at 7 A.M., placed in hot oven to bake at 20 minute intervals starting at 10:30 A.M., removed at same intervals starting at 11:15 A.M., pierced and sent to dining rooms for service starting at 11:30 A.M.
D. jelly omelet made by skillet method by cracking eggs early in morning, frying omelets at 10:30 A.M., spreading and folding jelly into them, cutting into standard portions, and placing them in a warm oven to hold for serving at 11:30 to 1 P.M.

15. Of the following, the LEAST important consideration in planning menus is the

15._____

A. facilities and equipment available for food preparation
B. ethnic and cultural food habits of patients
C. per capita budgetary allowance
D. method of food service to be used

16. In planning alternate choices of food items on a selective menu, it is MOST important to list alternatives which are of approximately the same

16._____

A. cost per portion
C. degree of acceptability

B. food grouping
D. color and texture

17. Many hospitals favor the use of cycle menus to improve their food service. However, cycle menus should NOT be used to

17._____

A. simplify menu writing
B. promote standardization of recipes and food production procedures

C. provide a fixed, unalterable menu pattern
D. help maintain better cost control

18. The one of the following which is LEAST useful in computing raw food costs for a given period is the

A. inventory records of foods received and issued
B. unit and total costs of foods used
C. records of overhead and salaries
D. record of meals served

19. The one of the following which has LEAST value in pre-costing a menu before it is served is the

A. desired portion size of each item
B. cost of the ingredients
C. cost of labor
D. estimated number of portions required

20. When planning menus, one should try to include items which are generally acceptable to as many individuals as possible to reduce leftovers.
Of the following, the food you should plan to use LEAST often in order to avoid excessive leftovers is

A. chicken a la king
B. roast beef
C. lettuce and tomato salad
D. chocolate layer cake

21. To maintain good standards of nutrition, the LARGEST percentage of the food dollar should be spent for

A. cereal products
B. fruits and vegetables
C. dairy products
D. meats

22. When giving diet instruction to a patient, the FIRST thing a dietitian should do is to

A. explain the essentials of an adequate diet
B. determine the amount of money available for food
C. determine present and previous patterns of eating
D. explain that a change in food habits will make the patient healthier

23. Assume that an older person asks for advice on how he can achieve greater enjoyment of meals and less distress after eating.
Of the following, the suggestion you should NOT make is that he eat

A. a good breakfast to start the day
B. four or five light meals instead of three heavier meals
C. mostly cereal products since these are easiest to prepare and masticate
D. the heaviest meal at noon rather than at night if sleeping is difficult

24. Of the following, the MOST desirable dinner menu for a geriatric patient who is on a regular diet is

A. grilled frankfurters, baked beans, cole slaw, baked apple
B. pot roast, noodles, carrot timbale, applesauce

C. fried chicken, mashed potatoes, rutabagas, cheese strudel
D. broiled fish, French fried potatoes, broccoli, cherry pie

25. Of the following menus, the one which is LEAST acceptable from the point of view of good menu planning for a patient on a regular diet is

A. roast lamb, mashed potatoes, buttered carrot rings, applesauce, bread and butter, cottage pudding with custard sauce, coffee, tea or milk
B. simmered corned beef, parsley buttered potatoes, steamed cabbage wedge, horseradish and beet relish, bread and butter, fresh fruit cup, coffee, tea, milk
C. Salisbury steak with mushroom gravy, French fried potatoes, sliced tomato salad on chicory, French dressing, vanilla ice cream, oatmeal cookie, coffee, tea, milk
D. baked cured ham with mustard sauce, scalloped sweet potatoes with apples, cole slaw, bread and butter, Boston cream pie, coffee, tea, milk

---

KEY (CORRECT ANSWERS)

1.	D	11.	A
2.	D	12.	D
3.	C	13.	B
4.	A	14.	C
5.	C	15.	D
6.	B	16.	B
7.	B	17.	C
8.	A	18.	C
9.	B	19.	D
10.	D	20.	A

21.	D
22.	C
23.	C
24.	B
25.	A

EXAMINATION SECTION TEST 1

DIRECTIONS: Each question or incomplete statement is followed by several suggested answers or completions. Select the one that BEST answers the question or completes the statement. *PRINT THE LETTER OF THE CORRECT ANSWER IN THE SPACE AT THE RIGHT.*

1. The one of the following groups of garnishes or accompaniments which is MOST appropriate for the entree designated is 1.____

   A. boiled beef; horseradish sour cream sauce, mixed pickles, beet and onion relish, lemon wedge
   B. roast veal; cranberry sauce, fried apple ring, parsley, French fried onion ring
   C. broiled fish; lemon wedge, tartar sauce, chopped parsley, lemon butter
   D. hamburger; sliced onion, catsup, French fried onion rings, Hollandaise sauce

2. Assume that the following menu has been submitted: chicken fricasee, mashed potatoes, cauliflower, bread and butter, applesauce, coffee, tea, milk. The CHIEF defect of this menu is that it is 2.____

   A. inadequate in protein content
   B. lacking in color and texture contrast
   C. improperly balanced as to nutrient content
   D. too high in calories

3. Assume that the following menu has been submitted for lunch: baked ham, pan browned parsnips, baked sweet potato, cornbread and butter, Apple Brown Betty with whipped topping. This menu is NOT well-planned primarily because 3.____

   A. there are too many calories
   B. there are no vitamin C foods
   C. there is not enough variety in texture of the foods
   D. the workload is not well distributed for the kitchen's cooking equipment

4. If a patient on a diabetic diet dislikes milk, he may exchange the milk with one 4.____

   A. bread exchange, one meat exchange, and one fat exchange
   B. fruit exchange
   C. bread exchange, one beverage, and one fat exchange
   D. meat exchange and one fruit exchange

5. The one of the following foods which can be used by a diabetic patient as a substitute in a meat exchange is 5.____

   A. ice cream
   B. cheddar cheese
   C. lima beans
   D. blackeye peas

6. Of the following foods, the one which should NOT be included in a clear liquid diet is 6.____

   A. milk
   B. fat-free broth
   C. fruit or vegetable juice
   D. carbonated beverages

2 (#1)

7. The one of the following which is permitted on a 500 mg. sodium diet is

A. cornflakes
B. rice krispies
C. puffed wheat
D. wheat flakes

8. The one of the following statements which is INCORRECT is that riboflavin

A. helps the cells utilize oxygen
B. helps keep vision clear
C. prevents cracking of mouth corners
D. helps the body absorb calcium

9. The one of the following which is NOT concerned with the digestion of fat is

A. cholecystokinin
B. lipase
C. bile
D. ptyalin

10. The diet which should be given to a patient who has chronic kidney disease with nitrogen retention is

A. high protein, low carbohydrate
B. low protein
C. low calcium, low phosphorus
D. low purine

11. The diet MOST likely to be ordered for the pernicious vomiting of pregnancy is

A. high carbohydrate, low fat
B. high carbohydrate, high fat, high protein
C. low carbohydrate, low fat, high protein
D. high protein, low sodium

12. In the treatment of hemorrhagic and nutritional anemias, the MOST important nutrients to stress are iron and

A. protein
B. vitamin A
C. iodine
D. vitamin E

13. The USUAL diet for a patient with acute gallbladder is a _____ diet.

A. low fat
B. 1000 mg. sodium
C. high protein
D. low cholesterol

14. Assume that a leukemia patient has difficulty swallowing the foods prescribed for her. In order to provide a diet which is nutritionally adequate, it is LEAST advisable to recommend

A. a liquid diet emphasizing high caloric liquids and protein supplements
B. nasal tube feeding in order to meet all nutritional requirements and to avoid the problem of swallowing
C. a diet on which the meat is minced and all fruits and vegetables are pureed
D. a diet similar to the one prescribed for her except that each item is pureed

15. The diet MOST likely to be prescribed for a patient who has renal stones is a(n) _____ diet.

A. elimination
B. low oxalate
C. low cholesterol
D. high carbohydrate, low protein, low fat

16. A rice diet is USUALLY prescribed for patients who

A. have high blood pressure
B. have a food allergy
C. are recovering from a gallbladder operation
D. require a high caloric intake

17. Patients suffering severe burns are MOST likely to have

A. loss of serum protein
B. steatorrhea
C. polyneuritis
D. stomatitis

18. Of the following statements concerning phenylketonuria, the one that is NOT correct is that it

A. is caused by an enzyme deficiency
B. leads to mental retardation
C. is treated by the restriction of carbohydrates
D. must be detected in the first few months of life in order to be treated

19. During all periods of growth, vitamin D is essential for efficient absorption and utilization of

A. calcium and potassium
B. potassium and iron
C. magnesium and calcium
D. phosphorus and calcium

20. In the treatment of urinary calculi, the one of the following which will assist in maintaining an acid urine is

A. cranberry juice
B. peas
C. cabbage
D. corn oil

21. Of the following, the food containing the HIGHEST amount of thiamine per 100 gram portion is

A. fresh green peas
B. fresh pork
C. fresh spinach
D. ground beef

22. The one of the following foods which is the POOREST source of niacin per 100 gram portion is

A. lean meats
B. peanuts
C. whole grain cereals
D. green leafy vegetables

23. Of the following lists of foods, the one which will contribute MOST to the ascorbic acid content of a diet is

A. potatoes, green peppers, raw cabbage
B. enriched bread, pork, turnips
C. whole wheat bread, potatoes, prunes
D. apples, dates, plums

24. Of the following foods, the content of unsaturated fatty acids is GREATEST in

A. butter
B. corn oil
C. beef suet
D. lard

4 (#1)

25. Of the following, the one with the LOWEST vitamin C content per 4 oz. portion is _____ juice.

A. orange
C. tomato

B. lemon
D. grapefruit

KEY (CORRECT ANSWERS)

1.	C	11.	A
2.	B	12.	A
3.	D	13.	A
4.	A	14.	C
5.	B	15.	B
6.	A	16.	A
7.	C	17.	A
8.	D	18.	C
9.	D	19.	D
10.	B	20.	A

21. B
22. D
23. A
24. B
25. C

TEST 2

DIRECTIONS: Each question or incomplete statement is followed by several suggested answers or completions. Select the one that BEST answers the question or completes the statement. *PRINT THE LETTER OF THE CORRECT ANSWER IN THE SPACE AT THE RIGHT.*

1. When roasting meat, the GREATEST yield of finished product may be expected when 1._____

   A. it is quickly seared on both sides at the beginning
   B. a high temperature is used throughout the roasting period
   C. a small quantity of water is added during roasting
   D. a low temperature is used throughout the roasting process

2. Of the following, the meat which is LEAST suitable for roasting is 2._____

   A. loin of pork · B. corned brisket
   C. rump of veal · D. leg of lamb

3. The loss of weight which results from braising boneless bottom round of beef, when proper techniques are used, is 3._____

   A. negligible · B. about 10%
   C. about 25% · D. over 50%

4. Of the following, the one which gives the MOST appropriate cooking temperature for the food indicated is 4._____

   A. beef loaf - $450°$ F · B. baked potatoes - $250°$ F
   C. caramel custard - $325°$ F · D. gingerbread - $475°$ F

5. In teaching a *cook trainee* how to deep fat fry various items of food, one should NOT instruct him to 5._____

   A. lower the food into the fat quickly
   B. make uniform portions of food for frying in the same load
   C. fill frying baskets to no more than 2/3 of capacity
   D. drain raw wet foods well before frying

6. Foods cooked incorrectly often lose flavor. When cooking beans or carrots, it is LEAST advisable to 6._____

   A. boil them in a small amount of water
   B. cook them in a steamer
   C. cook them in a pressure cooker
   D. cook them in an uncovered kettle

7. Of the following, the one which would make the LEAST satisfactory thickening agent in a casserole is 7._____

   A. wheat flour · B. rice
   C. cornstarch · D. tapioca

8. If baking powder biscuits do not rise to the proper height, the MOST probable cause is too 8._____

   A. *little* shortening · B. *much* handling of dough
   C. *little* flour · D. *much* baking powder

2 (#2)

9. A soggy bottom crust in a lemon meringue pie is MOST probably caused by

   A. handling the crust too much
   B. baking at too high a temperature
   C. refrigeration of the crust prior to baking
   D. pouring in the filling when the pie is hot

10. The MOST appropriate type of poultry to purchase for chicken a la king is

   A. fowl   B. roasters   C. fryers   D. broilers

11. Of the following, Grade B eggs may be used MOST satisfactorily for

   A. poaching   B. scrambling
   C. frying   D. coddling

12. Considering both quality and economy, the BEST choice of the following grades to be specified when ordering apples for sauce is

   A. fancy   B. extra fancy
   C. utility   D. U.S. #1

13. When submitting requisitions, the dietitian should give correct specifications for each item.
Of the following items, the one which is CORRECTLY specified is

   A. celery - fresh, Grade A, trimmed, in boxes, 140 pounds
   B. oranges - fresh, commercial grade, size 75 to the half crate, 225 pounds
   C. salad greens - romaine, fresh, Grade A, trimmed, 30 pounds
   D. onions - dry, Grade A, in sacks, 200 pounds

14. The one of the following specifications which is INCOMPLETE is

   A. 200 lbs. of ham, 10 to 12 lbs. each, U.S. #1
   B. 120 lbs. fresh bottom rounds, 20 to 30 lbs. each, Choice
   C. 250 lbs. of boneless corned brisket, deckel removed, 10 to 12 lbs. each, Good
   D. 225 lbs. double veal legs, cut short, 40 to 48 lbs. each, Choice

15. Of the following food items, the one which does NOT have the correct varieties listed for it is

   A. melon - Honeydew, Cantaloupe, Persian, Casaba
   B. potatoes - Idaho, Cobbler, Russet, Yam
   C. onions - Spanish, Bermuda, Yellow, Red
   D. apples - McIntosh, Emperor, Delicious, Concord

16. Assume that you plan to serve 500 portions of beef stew, with 3 ounces of cooked meat in each portion.
To provide this, you would need _____ lbs. _____ beef chuck.

   A. 95; boneless   B. 100; whole
   C. 125; boneless   D. 175; whole

3 (#2)

17. You are serving buttered carrot rings on a menu for which you need 750 servings. The number of pounds of topped carrots you should order is MOST NEARLY _____ lbs.

A. 50 B. 75 C. 150 D. 300

18. Frozen broccoli is on the menu for dinner and you require 260 servings. The number of 2 1/2 lb. packages you would need is MOST NEARLY

A. 10 B. 25 C. 50 D. 100

19. You wish to serve canned peas to 300 patients on the regular diet, 50 patients on bland diet, 35 patients on low fat diet, and 65 patients on light diet. Peas are supplied in #10 cans, and these are ordered by the case only. The number of cases you would need is

A. 1 B. 2 C. 3 D. 4

20. In order to ensure a minimum of leftover when you plan to serve 3 oz. portions of mashed potatoes to 500 persons, it would be BEST to order _____ potatoes.

A. 40 lbs. instant
B. 50 lbs. peeled
C. 2 cases #10 cans of whole
D. one 100 lb. sack of

21. The one of the following amounts which is MOST likely to yield 100 average servings is

A. dry prunes, 25 lbs.
B. bacon, sliced, rind removed (2 slices per serving), 20 lbs.
C. coffee, ground for drip, percolator or silex, 2 lbs.
D. egg noodles, buttered, 18 lbs.

22. The one of the following which would be INCORRECT to order when serving 200 persons is

A. 8 #10 cans of applesauce
B. 1 1/2 cases of #5 cans of tomato juice
C. 100 lbs. of eviscerated fowl
D. 20 lbs. of rice

23. To ensure that foods are relatively free of contamination when served in a cafeteria during a three hour meal period, it would be MOST advisable to

A. stagger periods of preparation and service to the counter
B. maintain a steam table temperature of $120°$ F
C. reheat foods when they cool down
D. eliminate all creamed foods from the menu

24. If egg salad has been prepared in a safe and sanitary manner, the criterion to be used to determine if it may be served one day later is that it

A. still tastes good
B. has a satisfactory general appearance
C. still smells good
D. has been continuously refrigerated

25. The one of the following statements concerning proper storage which is INCORRECT is that

A. crates of eggs should be stored upright, never on ends or sides, because eggs are packed with the small end down
B. crates of lettuce or fruit should not be stacked upright but on the side and should be cross-stacked to provide for air circulation
C. fresh raw meat such as veal carcass should be carefully wrapped when stored to prevent contamination
D. onions and potatoes do not require refrigeration; they are best stored in a dark, well-ventilated room at a temperature of 50° to 60° F

KEY (CORRECT ANSWERS)

1.	D		11.	B	
2.	B		12.	C	
3.	C		13.	C	
4.	C		14.	A	
5.	A		15.	D	
6.	D		16.	C	
7.	C		17.	C	
8.	B		18.	B	
9.	D		19.	C	
10.	A		20.	D	
		21.	C		
		22.	D		
		23.	A		
		24.	D		
		25.	C		

TEST 3

DIRECTIONS: Each question or incomplete statement is followed by several suggested answers or completions. Select the one that BEST answers the question or completes the statement. *PRINT THE LETTER OF THE CORRECT ANSWER IN THE SPACE AT THE RIGHT.*

1. Of the following, the one which gives the LEAST desirable temperature for storing the item indicated is

   A. ripe bananas - $60°$ to $70°$ F
   B. fresh eggs - $53°$ to $58°$ F
   C. salad greens - $40°$ to $45°$ F
   D. fresh lamb - $33°$ to $38°$ F

   1.____

2. Of the following, the MOST important reason for requiring good ventilation in a storeroom is to prevent

   A. condensation of moisture
   B. roach or rodent infestation
   C. complaints from storekeepers about odors
   D. spoilage of canned goods

   2.____

3. Of the following foods, the one which is LEAST susceptible to insect infestation is

   A. dried beans
   B. dried fruits
   C. plain gelatin
   D. non-fat dry milk

   3.____

4. Of the following, the MOST effective measure for the elimination of rodents in a hospital kitchen is to

   A. clean the floors every day
   B. spread poison once a month in all allowable areas
   C. eliminate harborages
   D. screen off the slop sinks at all times

   4.____

5. Of the following ways to store food, it is LEAST desirable to place

   A. sacks of dried beans on racks
   B. cans of peas on the floor
   C. packages of cereal on shelves
   D. quarters of lamb on hooks in the refrigerator

   5.____

6. The MOST important reason for NOT overcrowding refrigerators is to

   A. make cleaning easier
   B. allow air circulation to reach all foods
   C. prevent waste resulting from overlooked foods
   D. reduce opportunities for pilferage of food

   6.____

7. Cooked foods should be cooled and refrigerated quickly, PRIMARILY to

   A. *prevent* growth and development of bacteria
   B. *preserve* food nutrients

   7.____

C. *prevent* loss of moisture content
D. *preserve* a *fresh cooked* appearance

8. In planning the layout of a kitchen, it is MOST important to arrange for

A. grouping together of large pieces of equipment
B. a separate work area for each cook
C. a smooth and orderly flow of work
D. separation of *wet* and *dry* areas

9. Of the following, the MOST satisfactory work surface for a cook's work table is

A. hardwood 4" thick
B. heavy gauge stainless steel
C. heavy duty galvanized iron
D. heavy gauge aluminum

10. Of the following, the practice which is LEAST advisable in the operation and maintenance of a food grinder is to

A. hold the knife and plate in place by screwing the adjustment ring as tight as possible
B. use a mallet to push pieces of food into the grinder
C. remove the grinder plate and clean it thoroughly with a brush after each use
D. remove the grinder head at the end of the day and clean all loose parts before storing them

11. The MAIN reason for selecting a cafeteria counter of standard fabricated units rather than a custom-built counter of the same quality is the

A. lower initial cost
B. easier cleaning
C. greater flexibility for change and expansion
D. lower maintenance costs

12. Of the following, the MOST suitable steam equipment for a main kitchen in a 100 bed hospital is

A. one compartment steamer, one 80 gallon jacketed kettle, and one 60 gallon jacketed kettle
B. two 30 gallon jacketed kettles and one 20 gallon jacketed kettle
C. one 3 compartment steamer and two 30 gallon jacketed kettles
D. two 2 compartment steamers and one 20 gallon jacketed kettle

13. The BEST choice for the top of a kitchen work table is

A. 2 inch solid wood
B. 12 gauge monel metal
C. 20 gauge stainless steel
D. galvanized metal

3 (#3)

14. For equipment such as steam tables which require a water supply, it is MOST important to

A. make sure there are no submerged inlets
B. specify all stainless steel construction
C. provide a heat booster
D. supply both hot and cold water

15. In requisitioning a steam jacketed kettle, the LEAST important specification is that the

A. draw off tube should be as close to the kettle as possible
B. bottom should be pitched to facilitate run-off of contents
C. kettle should be wall hung for easier cleaning
D. draw off valve should be easily removable

16. The MAIN factor to consider when purchasing a slicing machine is the

A. ease of cleaning
B. adequacy of the safety guard for the cutting edge
C. size of the machine in relation to the volume of slicing
D. availability of replacement parts

17. In submitting your annual budget, you have requested a 2 drawer work table of complete stainless steel construction.
If you are told that you must request a less expensive model, the MOST acceptable compromise for you to make would be to

A. substitute ducoed legs with stainless steel feet
B. substitute drawers of galvanized metal with stainless steel fronts
C. specify a lighter weight stainless steel
D. reduce the size of the table

18. The one of the following which is MOST likely to yield 100 average servings is

A. fish filet - 30 pounds
B. cream for coffee - 6 quarts
C. oatmeal (rolled oats) - 5 pounds
D. frozen spinach - 10 pounds

19. The one of the following requisitions which is NOT correct for 600 servings is

A. 15 lbs. of ground coffee
B. 9 lbs. of margarine chips for toast
C. 3 #10 cans of jelly
D. 60 lbs. of granulated sugar for cereal

20. You have requisitioned 8000 lbs. of beef carcass (650 to 700 lbs. per carcass). This will yield tender steaks, tender roasts, and less tender cuts for roasting, stewing, and chopping.
Taking into account loss from trim, bones, and fat when the carcasses are processed, the amount of edible meat these carcasses should yield is MOST NEARLY _____ lbs.

A. 4500 B. 5360 C. 6500 D. 7120

4 (#3)

21. Analysis of the distribution of the average food dollar in a hospital can be of assistance to the dietitian in planning for and checking on the expenditure of funds. Of the following, the MOST advisable distribution of funds for categories of food is: meat, poultry, and fish _____%; dairy products _____%; fruits and vegetables _____%; bread and cereal _____%; miscellaneous _____%.

    A. 40; 20; 20; 10; 10
    B. 50; 10; 10; 10; 20
    C. 20; 20; 20; 20; 20
    D. 30; 30; 30; 5; 5

22. When planning a nutrition curriculum for the clinical instruction of student nurses, the factor which deserves the LEAST consideration is the

    A. educational purposes which the school of nursing seeks to attain
    B. educational experiences which are likely to meet the school's objectives
    C. service needs of the dietary department of the hospital
    D. methods of determining if the educational objectives have been attained

23. The current trend in the teaching of nutrition and diet therapy to student nurses emphasizes

    A. role playing and discussion groups as the most significant teaching devices
    B. instruction in food laboratories on preparation of foods
    C. instruction in food preparation and service to patients in the wards
    D. the clinical importance of diet therapy in a patient-centered plan of teaching

24. Suppose that the electric slicer used in the main kitchen is frequently out of order because of a short in the motor. The repair mechanic has demonstrated that this happens because excessive moisture is being used to flush out debris when cleaning the machine.
To prevent repetition of this breakdown, it would be MOST advisable to

    A. issue detailed written instructions on maintenance procedures to all cooks and kitchen employees who might have occasion to use or clean this slicer
    B. issue an order to all employees that no water is to be used when cleaning this slicer, only clean dry rags
    C. replace the slicer with a manual one that does not have a motor and, therefore, does not require electric current
    D. instruct two employees on each shift on the procedures to be used in cleaning the machine and restrict the use of the machine to them

25. Assume that a dietitian had instructed the kitchen helpers on how to minimize waste when preparing food for cooking. It would be MOST reasonable to conclude that such waste had been reduced subsequently if

    A. on a spot check, the employees observed were preparing the food as instructed
    B. operating costs for the dietary division during the next month were reduced
    C. the amount of food prepared during the next month decreased on a per capita basis
    D. requisitions of food supplies during the next month decreased

21.___

22.___

23.___

24.___

25.___

5 (#3)

KEY (CORRECT ANSWERS)

1. B	11. C
2. A	12. C
3. C	13. B
4. C	14. A
5. B	15. C
6. B	16. B
7. A	17. A
8. C	18. A
9. B	19. D
10. A	20. B

21. A
22. C
23. D
24. D
25. C

EXAMINATION SECTION TEST 1

DIRECTIONS: Each question or incomplete statement is followed by several suggested answers or completions.Select the one that BEST answers the question or completes the statement. *PRINT THE LETTER OF THE CORRECT ANSWER IN THE SPACE AT THE RIGHT.*

1. Assume that you have found that coffee served in the doctor's dining room is watery and has grounds in it.
Of the following, the BEST action for you to take is to

   A. complain to the employee who made the coffee
   B. check with the employee who was responsible for coffee preparation and review the current procedure for coffee making
   C. complain to the supplier about the inferior quality of the coffee
   D. ignore the situation

1.____

2. If the gelatin dessert planned for the evening meal did not congeal in time, it would be MOST advisable for you to

   A. serve it as is
   B. throw it away
   C. substitute another dessert
   D. omit dessert for this meal

2.____

3. Of the following, the LEAST necessary information required for a job analysis is

   A. an accurate description of the task to be performed
   B. the desired sequence and probable time required for each step taken
   C. qualifications of the workers on the job
   D. a list of the equipment to be used and the surroundings of the job

3.____

4. Of the following, the LEAST desirable procedure to follow in caring for an electric food cutter is to

   A. oil the machine once a day
   B. remove the guard, clean the knives and bowl after each using
   C. keep the machine covered when not in use
   D. be sure not to allow water to get into the motor while cleaning the machine

4.____

5. Of the following, the MOST desirable method for cleaning the meat block is to

   A. soak the entire block in soapy water, then rinse it clean
   B. use a steel scraper or brush, brush thoroughly, and dry wipe the block
   C. use sandpaper and wipe the block clean
   D. wipe it first with a dry cloth, then polish it with an oiled rag

5.____

6. The ADVANTAGE of using dry milk powder over whole milk is that it is

   A. time saving
   B. cheaper
   C. labor saving
   D. more nutritious

6.____

2 (#1)

7. A GOOD complement to a main dish of cheese is a

A. side dish of cold cuts B. broiled chop
C. crisp, green salad D. juicy roast

8. Raw fruits should be included when planning menus not only because of their vitamin and mineral content but also because of their

A. low residue content B. protein properties
C. high energy content D. laxative properties

9. Cereals are included in the daily menu MAINLY because

A. they contain proteins of high biological value
B. of their calcium content
C. they are a rich source of carbohydrates
D. of their rich supply of fats

10. Fish should be used at least once a week primarily because it is a GOOD source of

A. iron B. vitamin C
C. zinc D. iodine

11. Milk is pasteurized in order to

A. increase its fat content
B. destroy disease organisms
C. break up the fat globules
D. increase the vitamin content

12. Milk which has the fat globules dispersed throughout is known as

A. approved B. pasteurized
C. certified D. homogenized

13. Milk is often described as a complete food; however, it contains a POOR amount of

A. calcium B. iron C. protein D. vitamin A

14. To *purée* means to

A. cook in a small amount of fat
B. cut or chop fine
C. press through a sieve
D. tear in thin strips

15. To sauté is to

A. cook in hot fat
B. cook in oil deep enough to cover
C. pour fat over the food
D. fry lightly in a small amount of fat, turning frequently

16. French dressing will, upon standing, separate into two layers because it

A. does not contain an emulsifying agent
B. contains an emulsifying agent

C. was not thoroughly mixed
D. contains twice as much vinegar as oil

17. Cooking meats at a low temperature is CHIEFLY advisable because it results in 17.____

A. less shrinkage and greater palatability of the meat
B. a more well-done product
C. less waste of water and juices
D. more gravy

18. A method of cooking by dry heat is known as 18.____

A. blanching B. frying C. baking D. steaming

19. A soup made from two or three kinds of meat, highly seasoned and cleared, is known as 19.____

A. consomme B. bouillon C. chowder D. bisque

20. A pinch of soda added to green vegetables in cookery enhances the green color; however, this procedure is NOT recommended *mainly* because it 20.____

A. hardens the fibers
B. destroys the vitamins
C. prolongs the cooking
D. makes the vegetables less digestible

21. Meat is cooked PRIMARILY in order to 21.____

A. loosen the connective tissue
B. retain the vitamins
C. kill the bacteria
D. coagulate the blood

22. Cake flour is BEST suited for making cakes because it 22.____

A. contains more gluten
B. is more elastic
C. contains less gluten
D. has more water absorbing power

23. A baked custard becomes watery and lumpy if it is 23.____

A. not mixed thoroughly
B. cooked too long at too high a temperature
C. too sweet
D. too salty

24. Of the following types of cake, the one that *usually* does NOT contain any shortening is 24.____

A. chocolate cake B. angel food cake
C. spice cake D. gingerbread

25. Two cases of #5 grapefruit juice will contain _____ cans. 25.____

A. 6 B. 12 C. 24 D. 36

4 (#1)

26. The number of tablespoons in a standard cup is

A. 8   B. 12   C. 16   D. 18

27. Pork of choice quality has a _____ fat.

A. soft bright red color and brittle
B. cherry color and pink
C. grayish color and crumbly
D. soft grayish-pink color and white

28. *Good* beef should be

A. pink in color, have light yellow fat, and hard flesh
B. bright red in color, have creamy white fat, well-marbled, and firm flesh
C. cherry in color, have hard fat, and firm flesh
D. pink in color, have soft fat, and hard flesh

29. White potatoes are BEST stored in a

A. dark, cool, fairly dry place with ventilation
B. dry, light, well-ventilated place
C. cold, damp, well-ventilated place
D. damp, light, well-ventilated place

30. Hominy grits are made from

A. rice   B. wheat   C. corn   D. oats

31. Fruit juices are BEST classified as _____ beverages.

A. nourishing   B. reinforced
C. stimulating   D. concentrated

32. The CHIEF difference in the composition of cocoa and chocolate is their _____ content.

A. fat   B. vitamin
C. protein   D. carbohydrate

33. Of the following fruits, the one which is NOT low in fat content is

A. bananas   B. prunes
C. apricots   D. avocado pears

34. When toasting a piece of bread, the

A. protein is changed to proteose
B. fat is made more digestible
C. moisture is removed and the surface starch is changed to dextrin
D. carbohydrate is changed to glucose

35. The MOST important contribution of fruit in the diet is its

A. vitamin content   B. high caloric value
C. satiety value   D. acid reaction

5 (#1)

36. The number of calories that a diet consisting of 130 grams carbohydrates, 65 grams protein, and 50 grams fat will yield is

A. 980 B. 1230 C. 1555 D. 1880

37. The number of grams of protein that a normal, moderately active woman weighing 133 pounds would require daily is *approximately*

A. 54 B. 60 C. 68 D. 70

38. Eight grams of fat when oxidized will yield the SAME number of calories as _____ grams of _____.

A. eight; protein
B. twelve; carbohydrate
C. fourteen; protein
D. eighteen; carbohydrate

39. A pat of butter weighing 7 grams will give _____ calories.

A. 28 B. 63 C. 75 D. 81

40. Two teaspoons of sugar weighing 10 grams will yield _____ calories.

A. 16 B. 20 C. 40 D. 50

KEY (CORRECT ANSWERS)

1.	B	11.	B	21.	A	31.	A
2.	C	12.	D	22.	C	32.	A
3.	C	13.	B	23.	B	33.	D
4.	A	14.	C	24.	B	34.	C
5.	B	15.	D	25.	C	35.	A
6.	B	16.	A	26.	C	36.	B
7.	C	17.	A	27.	D	37.	B
8.	D	18.	C	28.	B	38.	D
9.	C	19.	A	29.	A	39.	B
10.	D	20.	B	30.	C	40.	C

TEST 2

DIRECTIONS: Each question or incomplete statement is followed by several suggested answers or completions. Select the one that BEST answers the question or completes the statement. *PRINT THE LETTER OF THE CORRECT ANSWER IN THE SPACE AT THE RIGHT.*

1. Of the following, the MOST recent one which is used to relieve patients of their crippling and painful rheumatic symptoms in arthritis is

A. insulin   B. thyroxin   C. bile   D. ACTH

2. The organism MOST commonly involved in food poisoning is the

A. streptococcus   B. staphylococcus
C. salmonella   D. cl. botulinum

3. Of the following, the one RICHEST in antiscorbutic vitamin is

A. citrus fruits   B. yeast
C. glandular organs   D. egg white

4. The anti-sterility vitamin is known as vitamin

A. B_1 B. B_2 C. E   D. K

5. Ergosterol, upon irradiation with ultraviolet light, may be converted to

A. glucose   B. vitamin D
C. glycine   D. glycogen

6. An INDISPENSABLE amino acid is

A. glycine   B. tyrosine
C. alanin   D. tryptophan

7. Of the following foods, the one which is a NATURAL source of vitamin D is

A. vegetables   B. whole grain cereal
C. fruits   D. egg yolks

8. The vitamin which influences the calcification of the bone is vitamin

A. B   B. C   C. D   D. E

9. Of the following foods, the ones RICHEST in thiamine are

A. peas, oatmeal, lean pork
B. celery, farina, bacon
C. oranges, cheese, turkey
D. carrots, tomatoes, beef

10. The chemical name for vitamin B_2 is

A. biotin   B. pyridoxine
C. nicotinic acid   D. riboflavin

2 (#2)

11. A protein which will maintain life and promote growth is known as a(n) _____ protein.

A. complete
B. incomplete
C. partially complete
D. partially incomplete

12. Gliadin is an example of a(n)

A. complete protein
B. protein hydrolysate
C. incomplete protein
D. good quality protein

13. The CHIEF protein in milk is

A. rennin
B. lactalbumin
C. glutin
D. casein

14. The protein content of milk and egg beverages may be increased by the addition of

A. bananas
B. lactose
C. protein hydrolysates
D. lanolac

15. The form in which carbohydrate is stored in the body is

A. glycogen
B. glucose
C. sucrose
D. dextrin

16. Iron is an indispensable constituent of the diet since it is necessary for the

A. synthesis of insulin
B. production of thyroid
C. production of bile
D. synthesis of hemoglobin

17. To meet the calcium requirement during pregnancy, it is recommended that the diet of a pregnant woman contain

A. at least two eggs daily
B. one quart of milk daily
C. a serving of liver twice weekly
D. at least two oranges daily

18. Lack of iodine in the diet may result in

A. gout
B. simple goiter
C. arthritis
D. diabetes

19. Egg yolk from a hard cooked egg is added to an infant's diet at the age of three months CHIEFLY to

A. compensate for the low iron content of milk
B. give bulk to the diet
C. add protein to the diet
D. compensate for the low fat content of milk

20. Water is important in the diet not only as a solvent and medium for chemical changes but also because it

A. regulates metabolism
B. regulates body temperature
C. stimulates cell respiration
D. stimulates hormone secretion

3 (#2)

21. In addition to human or cow's milk, an infant should be given as its FIRST additional supplement

A. puréed fruits
B. egg yolk
C. cod liver oil
D. sieved cereal

22. Leafy vegetables should be included in a reducing diet MAINLY because they are

A. low in carbohydrates
B. good sources of protein
C. high in fatty acids
D. good sources of calcium

23. combination raw vegetable salad may be given on a _____ diet.

A. low residue
B. soft
C. regular
D. bland

24. Clear soups and bouillon may be taken ad lib by patients on reducing and diabetic diets because they

A. contain large amounts of minerals
B. have no fuel value
C. contain fat which gives a satiety value to the foods
D. have good protein value

25. The characteristics of a reducing diet for an obese person are low in caloric value,

A. fat and carbohydrate; normal or high in protein, vitamins, and minerals
B. fat, carbohydrate, protein, and vitamins
C. vitamins and minerals; normal or high in carbohydrate
D. and high in fat

26. The use of mineral oil in low caloric diets should be discouraged because it

A. interferes with the absorption of all fat soluble vitamins
B. is completely digestible
C. contains 9 calories per gram
D. interferes with the absorption of sugar

27. The diet prescribed for atonic constipation is

A. *high* in bulk and fiber
B. *low* in fat and lubricants
C. *low* in bulk and fiber
D. *high* in sugar

28. The diet prescribed in Addison's disease is

A. *low* in sodium and high in potassium
B. *high* in potassium and low in carbohydrate
C. *high* in sodium chloride
D. *low* in sodium and potassium

29. Of the following foods, the one prescribed in generous amounts for a child with celiac disease is

A. oatmeal
B. potatoes
C. peaches
D. bananas

30. Kempner's rice diet for the treatment of hypertension must be supplemented with

A. protein and sodium
C. vitamins and iron

B. butter and fluids
D. fat and protein

KEY (CORRECT ANSWERS)

1.	D	11.	A	21.	C
2.	C	12.	C	22.	A
3.	A	13.	D	23.	C
4.	C	14.	C	24.	B
5.	B	15.	A	25.	A
6.	D	16.	D	26.	A
7.	D	17.	B	27.	A
8.	C	18.	B	28.	C
9.	A	19.	A	29.	D
10.	D	20.	B	30.	C

TEST 3

DIRECTIONS: Each question or incomplete statement is followed by several suggested answers or completions. Select the one that BEST answers the question or completes the statement. *PRINT THE LETTER OF THE CORRECT ANSWER IN THE SPACE AT THE RIGHT.*

1. Of the following foods, the one that a patient on a low sodium diet should AVOID is

A. lettuce   B. celery   C. apples   D. milk

2. In planning an alkaline ash diet, the foods that should be OMITTED are

A. apples and peaches   B. plums and cranberries
C. almonds and chestnuts   D. raisins and carrots

3. A soft diet is

A. high in fat
B. low in residue and readily digested
C. not readily digested
D. high in laxative properties

4. The ketogenic diet is

A. very high in fat and low in carbohydrate
B. inadequate in calories
C. high in carbohydrate and low in fat
D. adequate in calcium

5. Of the following foods, the one HIGHEST in purine is

A. dairy products   B. vegetables
C. glandular organs   D. fruits

6. Beriberi is a deficiency disease caused by the LACK of

A. carbohydrate   B. vitamin B_6
C. vitamin B_{12} D. thiamine

7. A deficiency in niacin will produce

A. anemia   B. tetany   C. pellagra   D. scurvy

8. Dialized milk is prescribed in certain diets CHIEFLY because it

A. is high in vitamins
B. contains practically no sodium
C. is high in minerals
D. contains a lot of sodium

9. Milk, cream, and eggs are ESPECIALLY valuable in the treatment of peptic ulcers because they

A. increase the secretion of hydrochloric acid
B. are alkaline forming
C. have laxative properties
D. lower the gastric acidity

2 (#3)

10. The Grollman diet is used CHIEFLY for treating

A. hypertension
B. jaundice
C. diarrhea
D. ulcers

10._____

11. A patient who is allowed only water, clear tea, black coffee, and clear broth is said to be on a _____ fluid diet.

A. surgical
B. fortified
C. unrestricted
D. full

11._____

12. Of the following foods, the one which a patient sensitive to wheat must AVOID is

A. puffed rice
B. milk
C. gelatin
D. malted milk

12._____

13. Of the following foods, the one which a patient on a wheat-free diet may eat is

A. rye bread
B. vegetables with a cream sauce
C. rye krisp
D. bran muffins

13._____

14. Gelatinization is BEST defined as

A. swelling of gelatin in cold water
B. coagulation of gelatin
C. coagulation of starch
D. swelling of starch granules in hot water

14._____

15. The symbol A.P., as used in recipes and nutritional charts, means

A. always prepared
B. available protein
C. as purchased
D. always present

15._____

16. The symbol E.P., appearing in nutritional value food charts, stands for

A. easily purchased
B. edible portion
C. energy performed
D. easily prepared

16._____

17. In writing patients' orders, doctors often use symbols. If a doctor prescribed nourishment for a patient *t.i.d.*, it would mean that the patient was to receive nourishment

A. once a day
B. three times a day
C. twice a day
D. as desired

17._____

18. The enzyme which brings about the curdling of milk is called

A. rennin
B. ptyalin
C. bile
D. pepsin

18._____

19. Of the following food sources, the one RICHEST in cholesterol is

A. potatoes
B. mackerel
C. egg yolk
D. oranges

19._____

3 (#3)

20. The enzyme in saliva which acts on starch is called

A. rennin B. pepsin C. trypsin D. ptyalin

21. An overdose of insulin is LIKELY to produce

A. nervousness, excessive hunger, weakness, and sweating
B. vomiting, labored respiration, and anorexia
C. polyuria, restlessness, and anhydremia
D. nausea, labored respiration, and dyspnea

22. One unit of regular insulin will oxidize *approximately*

A. 2 gms. carbohydrate B. 2 gms. protein
C. 3 gms. fat D. 4 gms. carbohydrate

23. Insulin is a hormone derived from

A. alpha cells of the pancreas
B. beta cells of the Islands of Langerhans
C. bile
D. thyroid

24. To restore refined wheat flour to approximately the same nutrient level that it was before the flour was milled, the two important nutrients that are added are

A. calcium and phosphorus B. calcium and vitamin D
C. iodine and vitamin A D. iron and vitamin B

25. Incomplete combustion of fats produces a condition known as

A. cyanosis B. avitaminosis
C. ketosis D. anoxia

26. Inflammation of the kidneys is known as

A. nephritis B. achlorhydria
C. gastritis D. jaundice

27. The removal of the nitrogen group from the amino acid molecule is called

A. deaminization B. metabolism
C. nutrition D. absorption

28. One of the MOST important functions of the liver is to

A. convert carotene to vitamin C
B. form bile salts
C. produce thyroxine
D. maintain the normal composition of the blood

29. In essential hypertension, there is a(n)

A. *increase* in systolic pressure and a decrease in diastolic pressure
B. *decrease* in systolic pressure and an increase in diastolic pressure
C. *increase* in both systolic and diastolic pressure
D. *decrease* in both systolic and diastolic pressure

30. The glucose tolerance test is a test used to diagnose

A. ulcers
B. hypertension
C. gallbladder disease
D. diabetes

KEY (CORRECT ANSWERS)

#	Answer	#	Answer	#	Answer
1.	D	11.	A	21.	A
2.	B	12.	D	22.	A
3.	B	13.	C	23.	B
4.	A	14.	B	24.	D
5.	C	15.	C	25.	C
6.	D	16.	B	26.	A
7.	C	17.	B	27.	A
8.	B	18.	A	28.	B
9.	D	19.	C	29.	C
10.	A	20.	D	30.	D

EXAMINATION SECTION TEST 1

DIRECTIONS: Each question or incomplete statement is followed by several suggested answers or completions. Select the one that BEST answers the question or completes the statement. *PRINT THE LETTER OF THE CORRECT ANSWER IN THE SPACE AT THE RIGHT.*

1. The one of the following which is the MOST important requirement of a good menu is that it

   A. include a large variety of food
   B. list foods which are well-liked
   C. be printed neatly on a clean menu card
   D. be suited to the purpose for which it is planned

1.____

2. Of the following, the procedure which is MOST desirable for proper tray service is to

   A. heat all dishes before placing them on the tray
   B. serve hot food hot, and cold food cold
   C. have all patients elevated in order to permit easier swallowing of food
   D. always serve iced water on the tray

2.____

3. The PROPER position for the knife on the tray is

   A. above the dinner plate
   B. across the bread and butter plate
   C. to the right of the dinner plate
   D. next to the fork

3.____

4. For attractive tray service, it is MOST advisable to serve harvard beets

   A. on the plate with the meat
   B. in a small side vegetable dish
   C. on a bed of shredded lettuce
   D. with a very thick, heavy sauce

4.____

5. The kitchen dietitian can work MOST efficiently if her office is located

   A. away from the kitchen, so she can be free from distractions
   B. in a central position where she may view all that happens
   C. at the entrance to the kitchen where she can see people entering and leaving
   D. next to the pantry, so she can see that no unauthorized person enters

5.____

6. The PRIMARY purpose of keeping records in the dietary department is to

   A. reduce waste in ordering food and supplies
   B. increase consumption of the most nutritious foods
   C. train subordinates in office techniques
   D. maintain statistical records of retail prices

6.____

2 (#1)

7. A budget is BEST described as a(n)

   A. detailed plan for expenditures
   B. schedule for figuring depreciation of equipment over a period of years
   C. order for necessary equipment
   D. periodic accounting for past expenditures

8. Of the following, the CHIEF reason why a refrigerator door should NOT be left open is that the open door will

   A. stop the motor
   B. cause a drop in room temperature
   C. permit the cold air to rise to the top
   D. permit warm air to enter the refrigerator

9. Ovens with thermostatic heat controls should be

   A. kept closed at all times
   B. opened carefully to prevent jarring
   C. checked periodically for accuracy
   D. disconnected when not in use

10. The term *net weight* means MOST NEARLY the

    A. actual weight of an item
    B. weight of the container when empty
    C. combined weight of an item and its container
    D. estimated weight of the container alone

11. In requisitioning food, it is LEAST necessary for a dietitian to

    A. specify the exact quantity desired
    B. secure the signature of the cashier
    C. know the delivery times and order accordingly
    D. know the sizes in which foods are marketed

12. When receiving an order of food, it is INADVISABLE for the dietitian to

    A. check carefully against the order or requisition
    B. see that all fresh foods are weighed and checked in at the receiving room
    C. check for quality as well as quantity of foods delivered
    D. subtract two pounds tare from the weight of each package delivered in an order

13. Assume that, when inspecting a delivery of vegetables, you find a large amount of sorrel mixed in with a bushel of spinach.
The one of the following actions which it is MOST advisable for you to take is to

    A. sort the spinach and sorrel in cleaning and cook them separately to allow greater variety in the menu
    B. discard the sorrel as waste
    C. call the purchasing office and arrange to return the spinach as unsatisfactory
    D. place the sorrel in the refrigerator and return it to the driver on his next delivery

7.___
8.___
9.___
10.___
11.___
12.___
13.___

14. When purchasing iceberg lettuce, it is ADVISABLE to look for lettuce which is

A. loosely headed, with soft curly leaves and a yellow heart
B. tightly headed, elongated, with coarse green leaves
C. tightly headed, with medium green outside leaves and a pale green heart
D. loosely headed, with elongated stalk and rugged curly leaves

15. The term *30-40 prunes* is used to describe the

A. number of prunes in a box
B. particular variety of prunes
C. brand name of prunes
D. number of prunes in a pound

16. When ordering chocolate liquor, the dietitian should expect to receive a _____ chocolate.

A. solid piece of
C. liquid
B. semi-liquid
D. glass jar of

17. Of the following, the BEST reason for discarding the green part of potatoes is that it contains a poison known as

A. cevitamic acid
C. solanine
B. citric acid
D. trichinae

18. The number of cans that a standard case of #10 canned apples USUALLY contains is

A. 6
B. 12
C. 18
D. 24

19. Of the following, the person MOST closely associated with work in the field of infant behavior and feeding is

A. H. Pollack
C. E.J. Stieglitz
B. A. Gesell
D. J.F. Freeman

20. Of the following, the person BEST known for work in the field of diabetes is

A. N. Jolliffe
C. R.M. Wilder
B. H. Sherman
D. F. Stern

21. An egg which is strictly fresh will

A. float in cold water
B. have a thin and watery egg white
C. have a swollen egg yolk which is easily broken
D. sink in cold water

22. Cocoa and chocolate are rich in

A. glycogen
B. gum
C. cellulose
D. starch

23. The percentage of protein that is usually converted into glucose in the body is MOST NEARLY

A. 49%
B. 58%
C. 67%
D. 78%

4 (#1)

24. Of the following vegetables, the one which gives the LARGEST yield, pound for pound, when pureed is

A. fresh celery
C. frozen asparagus
B. frozen peas
D. fresh carrots

25. If the composition of two small rib chops is Protein - 21 grams and Fat - 17 grams, the number of calories in the two chops is MOST NEARLY

A. 136
B. 200
C. 237
D. 257

KEY (CORRECT ANSWERS)

1.	D	11.	B
2.	B	12.	D
3.	C	13.	C
4.	B	14.	C
5.	B	15.	D
6.	A	16.	C
7.	A	17.	C
8.	D	18.	A
9.	C	19.	B
10.	A	20.	C

21.	D
22.	D
23.	B
24.	D
25.	C

TEST 2

DIRECTIONS: Each question or incomplete statement is followed by several suggested answers or completions. Select the one that BEST answers the question or completes the statement. *PRINT THE LETTER OF THE CORRECT ANSWER IN THE SPACE AT THE RIGHT.*

1. An APPROPRIATE substitute for sucrose for a patient on a low carbohydrate diet is 1._____

A. saccharin   B. casec   C. lactose   D. protinol

2. Of the following, the vegetables which are high in protein and, therefore, sometimes substituted for meat are 2._____

A. green leafy vegetables   B. legumes
C. root vegetables   D. gourds

3. When planning menus, it is *advisable* to use fish at least once a week because it is a GOOD source of 3._____

A. iron   B. vitamin C   C. zinc   D. iodine

4. Of the following, the one which is a *non-nutritive* beverage is 4._____

A. clear tea   B. orangeade
C. oatmeal gruel   D. cream soda

5. Macaroni is *usually* used as a substitute for 5._____

A. salad   B. meat   C. potato   D. dessert

6. Bread is dextrinized by 6._____

A. toasting   B. chopping
C. drying in open air   D. soaking in hot water

7. Baked custard is used on the menu CHIEFLY 7._____

A. as a source of vitamin C
B. because of its high protein content
C. to add color
D. as a source of starch

8. The one of the following which is a *non-irritating* food is 8._____

A. cabbage   B. pickles   C. spaghetti   D. celery

9. Leaves of rhubarb and beets, when boiled in an aluminum container, will clean the container because they contain 9._____

A. sulphuric acid   B. oxalic acid
C. ammonia   D. alkali

10. When refinishing a refrigerator ice cube tray, the one of the following which should NOT be used as a coating material is 10._____

A. aluminum   B. cadmium   C. tin   D. nickel

2 (#2)

11. The Department of Health requires the sterilization of eating utensils by

    A. hot air sterilizers
    B. ultraviolet rays
    C. chemical solutions
    D. water at 180° F

12. Suppose that the dishwashing machine has become clogged with food particles. Of the following, the action which would be MOST advisable for the dietitian to take *first* is to

    A. call the service man to disassemble and clean the machine
    B. instruct the employees assigned to washing dishes about proper scraping of dishes
    C. order the employees to prerinse all dishes in order to prevent clogging
    D. remove the strainer tray

13. The one of the following which is the MOST effective way to rid a food storeroom of mice is to

    A. cement tight all holes which permit invasion
    B. set traps to catch the mice
    C. spread poison around the floor
    D. burn a sulphur candle in the storeroom

14. Black stoves are cleaned BEST by

    A. polishing with an oiled cloth
    B. rubbing with a piece of wax paper
    C. scrubbing with soap and water
    D. heating until they are red hot

15. Of the following, the BEST procedure for cleaning a red quarry tile floor in a hospital kitchen is to

    A. scrub it, then wax the floor
    B. hose it down with steam
    C. wash it with a strong soap
    D. wash it with a lye

16. After making ice cream, it is MOST important that the machine be

    A. rinsed thoroughly in cold water
    B. sterilized
    C. soaked in soap solution
    D. scrubbed with a brush

17. A dietitian assigned to work with clinic patients should have a basic knowledge of the foods of foreign-born people. Of the following, the MOST important reason for this is that

    A. it is interesting and exciting to eat the exotic dishes of foreign lands
    B. such knowledge would prove beyond doubt that poor diet is the cause of poor health among the foreign-born

C. such knowledge would help the dietitian to plan the patient's prescribed diet around familiar foods
D. many foreign dishes are more nutritious than American foods

18. The clinic dietitian meets several problems of the aging. The one of the following for which she is LEAST responsible is the

A. detection of the onset of chronic degenerative diseases
B. conservation of the health of the individual
C. re-evaluation of the caloric requirements of aged patients
D. overcoming of superstitions and food fallacies

19. When advising on methods of economizing, the clinic dietitian should instruct patients to AVOID buying

A. foods in quantity, even though storage space permits
B. foods that are in season and in abundance on the market
C. less expensive cuts of meat
D. butter, since there are less expensive substitutes on the market

20. The one of the following services which is the LEAST basic function of a nutrition clinic is to

A. serve as a teaching center for students
B. provide educational programs for patients of all ages
C. follow up the nutritional status of individual patients
D. secure diet histories of patients for the correction of undesirable food habits

21. Time and motion studies in the field of dietetics are used PRIMARILY to

A. check on lateness and absence records of employees
B. reduce effort and increase efficiency in performing particular tasks
C. prepare estimates of time required between requisition and delivery dates
D. schedule the daily work assignments for the entire staff

22. The PRIMARY purpose of using standardized recipes is to

A. aid in controlling food costs
B. encourage the cooks to try out new foods
C. prepare large quantities of food
D. determine the caloric values of foods

23. The CHIEF advantage of keeping a perpetual inventory of stock items is that

A. supplies may be stored more easily
B. there will be less breakage and loss of stock
C. it makes it unnecessary to order replacements for stock supplies
D. the balance on hand at any time is easily determined

24. In order to prevent the loss of vitamins in cooking, it is HOST advisable to

A. cover the food completely with water while cooking and boil it rapidly
B. peel and soak vegetables in cold water before cooking

C. dice vegetables into small pieces and boil them in an open pot
D. cook vegetables in the shortest possible time in a covered pot containing little water

25. To marinate is to

A. let foods stand in a specially prepared liquid to add flavor or to tenderize them
B. cook food in liquid just below the boiling point
C. moisten food while cooking by pouring over it drippings or other liquids
D. cook food in water at boiling temperature

KEY (CORRECT ANSWERS)

1.	A	11.	D
2.	B	12.	A
3.	D	13.	A
4.	A	14.	C
5.	C	15.	B
6.	A	16.	B
7.	B	17.	C
8.	C	18.	A
9.	B	19.	D
10.	B	20.	A

21.	B
22.	A
23.	D
24.	D
25.	A

EXAMINATION SECTION

TEST 1

DIRECTIONS: Each question or incomplete statement is followed by several suggested answers or completions. Select the one that BEST answers the question or completes the statement. *PRINT THE LETTER OF THE CORRECT ANSWER IN THE SPACE AT THE RIGHT.*

1. Foods which are left over may be used by the menu planner CHIEFLY to
   - A. baste meats
   - B. stock the freezer with emergency supplies
   - C. provide more variety in the next day's menu
   - D. add minerals to the diet

2. When a recipe calls for cooking in a hot oven, it is MOST desirable to set the thermostat at a Fahrenheit temperature of
   - A. 300°
   - B. 350°
   - C. 425°
   - D. 525°

3. Of the following, the MOST satisfactory method for cooking the less tender cuts of meat is by
   - A. roasting
   - B. broiling
   - C. dry heat
   - D. moist heat

4. A two-pound chicken is BEST prepared by
   - A. broiling
   - B. stewing
   - C. baking
   - D. roasting

5. Fats are used in food preparation, *not only* as emulsifiers, *but also* as
   - A. shortening agents
   - B. leavening agents
   - C. catalysts
   - D. sweetening agents

6. Baking powder is used in cake mixtures CHIEFLY in order to
   - A. improve the flavor
   - B. increase the acidity
   - C. lighten the cake and increase its volume
   - D. hold the other ingredients together

7. When making a sponge cake, it is important to remember to
   - A. beat the batter until it doubles in bulk
   - B. bake the cake in an ungreased tube pan
   - C. bake the cake in a hot oven
   - D. remove the cake from the pan as soon as it is baked

8. When making pastry, the fat should be
   - A. creamed with the flour
   - B. first melted and then creamed with the flour
   - C. cut into the flour
   - D. added to the flour after the water is stirred in

9. Of the following, the procedure which is MOST advisable when cooking dried prunes is to
   - A. soak the fruit in hot water to seal in the juices
   - B. keep the uncooked fruit under refrigeration at all times
   - C. simmer the fruit slowly until it is tender
   - D. add sugar to the fruit to improve the flavor

10. Assume that you plan to serve a gelatin dessert for dinner. You have found that gelatin made in the usual way softens in hot weather.
Of the following, the procedure which is MOST advisable to follow on a warm day is to
    A. thicken the gelatin with cornstarch
    B. substitute a non-gelatin dessert
    C. use fruit juice in the mixture
    D. use less water than usual

11. When preparing cream of tomato soup, it is MOST advisable to
    A. add hot milk slowly to cold tomato juice
    B. mix milk and tomato juice and then heat
    C. add cold tomato juice slowly to hot milk
    D. add cold milk slowly to hot tomato juice

12. In order to prevent cornstarch from lumping in cooking, it is MOST advisable to
    A. mix the starch with cold liquid before heating
    B. add hot liquid immediately to the starch
    C. brown the starch and add hot liquid
    D. heat the starch in a double boiler

13. Of the following, the LEAST desirable way to dry bread is to place it in
    A. uncovered pans on top of heated ovens
    B. paper bags which are suspended over the stoves
    C. deep pans in a warm oven
    D. cabinets which have slow heat

14. Of the following, the one which is a mollusk used in the preparation of soup is
    A. crab   B. oyster   C. lobster   D. cod

15. Whole dry milk is preferable to evaporated milk for use as a beverage CHIEFLY because it
    A. takes less time to prepare
    B. contains more vitamins
    C. can be made to look and taste more like whole milk
    D. contains more calories

16. The one of the following which is a RESIDUE-FREE food is
    A. milk   B. grapefruit sections
    C. lettuce   D. lemon gelatin

17. The one of the following which is NOT a legume is
    A. peanuts   B. okra   C. beans   D. lentils

18. Of the following, the sugar which is SWEETEST is
    A. lactose   B. fructose   C. sucrose   D. maltose

19. Broths are of value in the diet CHIEFLY because they are
    A. high in food value
    B. a good source of protein
    C. effective appetite stimulants
    D. a good source of carbohydrates

20. Of the following groups, the one which may be served on a SOFT diet is
    A. cream soup, mashed potato, spinach purée, toast, butter, custard
    B. broiled chicken, mashed potato, buttered peas, toast, milk
    C. vegetable soup, lamp chops, mashed potato, lettuce salad, toast
    D. clear broth, baked potato, tenderloin steak, carrots, apple pie

21. Of the following fruits, those which may be included in a HIGH ACID ash diet are
    A. prunes   B. oranges   C. bananas   D. pears

22. Of the following statements regarding yeast, the one which is MOST accurate is that yeast
    A. is generally harmful   B. changes starch to sugar
    C. lives without air   D. requires alcohol to live

23. The souring of milk is due PRIMARILY to the action of bacteria on
    A. fatty acids   B. proteins   C. amino acids   D. lactose

24. Glycerol, which is an end product of fat metabolism, is further oxidized in the body to
    A. sucrose   B. galactose   C. levulose   D. glucose

25. Cereals should be included in menus that are planned PRIMARILY to be
    A. weight reducing   B. low in starch
    C. low in cost   D. high in vitamin C

KEY (CORRECT ANSWERS)

1. C		11. C	
2. C		12. A	
3. D		13. A	
4. A		14. B	
5. A		15. C	
6. C		16. D	
7. B		17. B	
8. C		18. B	
9. C		19. C	
10. D		20. A	
	21. A		
	22. B		
	23. D		
	24. D		
	25. C		

TEST 2

DIRECTIONS: Each question or incomplete statement is followed by several suggested answers or completions. Select the one that BEST answers the question or completes the statement. *PRINT THE LETTER OF THE CORRECT ANSWER IN THE SPACE AT THE RIGHT.*

1. Of the following, a high blood sugar content is MOST likely to be a symptom of
   A. anemia   B. diabetes mellitus
   C. arteriosclerosis   D. hypertension

2. Trichinosis is a disease which may be caused by
   A. eating ham which has been overcooked
   B. unsanitary handling of frozen meats
   C. eating food which has been contaminated by infected flies
   D. eating infected pork which has been cooked insufficiently

3. Of the following, the bacteria which causes MOST food poisoning cases is
   A. botulinum   B. salmonella   C. pneumococci   D. streptococci

4. In the normal diet, liver should be used at least once a week since it is a GOOD source of
   A. vitamin C   B. phosphorus   C. iron   D. roughage

5. Water is important in the daily intake of the body CHIEFLY because it
   A. causes the oxidation of food in the body
   B. is a transporting medium for all body substances
   C. cools the air in the lungs
   D. gives off minerals when it is digested

6. Cod liver oil is given to children CHIEFLY in order to aid in
   A. absorption of calcium   B. carbohydrate metabolism
   C. prevention of beriberi   D. regulation of osmotic pressure

7. Of the following statements with respect to the nutritional needs of children, the one which is MOST accurate is that
   A. a child of four years of age requires a minimum of 2000 calories a day
   B. it is better for a child to be slightly underweight than to be overweight
   C. proportionately, children require more protein per pound of body weight than do adults
   D. a child whose diet is deficient in vitamin D may develop scurvy as a result

8. The one of the following desserts which it is MOST advisable to use in a low protein diet is
   A. prune soufflé   B. fruit cup
   C. gelatin   D. junket

2 (#2)

9. The Karell diet is used in the care of
A. Addison's disease   B. cardiac conditions
C. diabetes   D. jaundice

9.___

10. Rowe elimination diets are used in cases involving
A. allergy   B. lead poisoning
C. constipation   D. nephritis

10.___

11. Of the following conditions, the one for which the normal diet is MODIFIED by restricting sodium is
A. tuberculosis B. diabetes   C. gastritis   D. edema

11.___

12. The one of the following conditions which may cause jaundice is
A. faulty functioning of the kidneys
B. an obstruction in the common bile duct
C. a deficiency of vitamin C
D. the presence of the yeast spore

12.___

13. It is GENERALLY accepted that exophthalmic goiter may result from
A. the inability of the body to metabolize purines
B. injury to the pancreas
C. a diet deficient in iodine
D. lack of sufficient sunlight and milk

13.___

14. Faulty ossification of the legs, ribs, and cranial bones are symptoms GENERALLY associated with
A. pellagra   B. rickets   C. neuritis   D. encephalitis

14.___

15. Of the following diseases, the one which is characterized PRIMARILY by destruction of the liver cells is
A. diabetes   B. leukemia   C. scurvy   D. cirrhosis

15.___

Questions 16-25.

DIRECTIONS: Column I lists 10 diseases or conditions, numbered 16 to 25, which require dietary treatment. Column II lists the dietary treatments which are generally used for the conditions listed in Column I. In the space at the right, opposite the number preceding each of the conditions in Column I, place the letter preceding the dietary treatment in Column II which is MOST appropriate for the condition in Column I.

COLUMN I	COLUMN II	
16. Addison's disease	A. low carbohydrate diet	16.___
17. cirrhosis	B. high caloric, non-stimulating diet	17.___
18. diabetes	C. non-residue diet, high in protein and acid ash	18.___
19. exophthalmic goiter		19.___
20. gastric ulcer	D. diet high in vitamin C and magnesium	20.___

3 (#2)

COLUMN I (cont'd)

21. gout
22. lipoid nephrosis
23. obesity
24. rickets
25. typhoid fever

COLUMN II (cont'd)

E. high protein, high carbohydrate, low roughage diet

F. high caloric, soft diet, given in small, frequent feedings

G. diet high in carbohydrate and vitamins, low in potassium, with added salt

H. diet with normal or high protein, vitamins, and minerals; low in fat and carbohydrate; low in caloric value

I. high protein and sulphur diet

J. low protein, purine-free diet

K. high protein, low fat diet, with limited sodium

L. diet high in protein and carbohydrate, low in fat, high in vitamin B complex

M. diet high in vitamin D

KEY (CORRECT ANSWERS)

1. B		11. D	
2. D		12. B	
3. B		13. C	
4. C		14. B	
5. B		15. D	
6. A		16. G	
7. C		17. L	
8. B		18. A	
9. B		19. B	
10. A		20. F	
	21. J		
	22. K		
	23. H		
	24. M		
	25. E		

EXAMINATION SECTION

TEST 1

DIRECTIONS: Each question or incomplete statement is followed by several suggested answers or completions. Select the one that BEST answers the question or completes the statement. *PRINT THE LETTER OF THE CORRECT ANSWER IN THE SPACE AT THE RIGHT.*

1. The item that acts as a catalytic agent for the assimilation of calcium and phosphorus is
   A. vitamin D   B. fat   C. vitamin B   D. protein   1.___

2. Contributing MOST to the weight of the living human body is
   A. copper   B. sodium   C. calcium   D. iron   2.___

3. Before cooking, the vegetable that MUST be soaked in water is
   A. string beans   B. Brussels sprouts
   C. turnips   D. celery   3.___

4. Amino acids are absorbed MAINLY in the
   A. stomach   B. liver   C. pancreas   D. intestine   4.___

5. Little spoilage occurs in stored, sun-dried fruits because the
   A. microorganisms have been destroyed
   B. moisture content is low
   C. pectin is inactive
   D. yeasts do not flourish in the absence of light   5.___

6. In pickling, the concentrated brine
   A. softens the cellulose
   B. preserves the original color
   C. retards the growth of microorganisms
   D. increases the acid content   6.___

7. Cheese is rich in
   A. calcium   B. iron   C. sodium   D. potassium   7.___

8. Tenderized dried fruits have been
   A. sulphurized, dried, then partially cooked
   B. dried, partially cooked, then partially dried
   C. partially cooked, dried, then partially cooked
   D. dried, sulphurized, then partially cooked   8.___

9. The MOST tender cuts of beef are from the
   A. loin and rib   B. leg and rib
   C. shoulder and loin   D. rump and neck   9.___

10. In anabolism, the number of calories yielded by one gram of carbohydrates is
    A. two   B. four   C. six   D. eight   10.___

2 (#1)

11. When making yeast rolls, the milk is scalded to
    A. improve the flavor of the product
    B. reduce the size of the air holes
    C. destroy the microorganisms
    D. encourage development of the yeast

12. Deterioration of dried vegetables is retarded by
    A. marinating before drying
    B. storage in metal boxes
    C. pre-cooking before drying
    D. infra-red light treatment before packaging

13. The LARGEST percentage of gluten is found in flour made from
    A. rye   B. barley   C. oats   D. wheat

14. A bed roll is a support for the patient's
    A. head   B. knees   C. back   D. feet

15. One pound of dried eggs is equivalent to ____ eggs.
    A. 50-60   B. 30-40   C. 20-25   D. 15-18

16. To store eggs at home,
    A. keep them exposed on the cupboard
    B. wash and place them in the refrigerator
    C. do not wash and place them in the refrigerator
    D. place them in a moderately cool place

17. Disease is MOST commonly spread through
    A. clothing   B. dishes   C. food   D. contact

18. For everyday use, the Fahrenheit temperature of the refrigerator should be
    A. $20°-25°$ B. $35°-40°$ C. $45°-50°$ D. $55°-60°$

19. To retard spoilage of bread, baking companies may add sodium
    A. benzoate   B. propionate
    C. sulphathionate   D. hypophosphate

20. Essential to jelly-making is
    A. proto-pectin   B. pectin
    C. pectic acid   D. pectoral liquor

KEY (CORRECT ANSWERS)

1.	A	11.	D
2.	C	12.	C
3.	B	13.	D
4.	D	14.	B
5.	B	15.	B
6.	C	16.	C
7.	A	17.	D
8.	B	18.	B
9.	A	19.	B
10.	B	20.	B

TEST 2

DIRECTIONS: Each question or incomplete statement is followed by several suggested answers or completions. Select the one that BEST answers the question or completes the statement. *PRINT THE LETTER OF THE CORRECT ANSWER IN THE SPACE AT THE RIGHT.*

1. A MAJOR source of riboflavin is
   A. meat   B. whole grains
   C. fruits   D. milk
   1.___

2. In wheat, the vitamin B complex is in the
   A. endosperm   B. aleuron layer
   C. bran   D. germ
   2.___

3. The duration of infectious colds has been materially diminished by dosages of vitamin
   A. A   B. B_1 C. B_2 D. E
   3.___

4. Yeast plants grow BEST at the Fahrenheit temperature of
   A. 70°-75°   B. 80°-85°   C. 90°-95°   D. 100°-105°
   4.___

5. A characteristic of riboflavin deficiency is
   A. cheilosis   B. catarrh   C. otitis   D. pellagra
   5.___

6. Anemia responds to
   A. ascorbic acid   B. folic acid
   C. niacin   D. carotene
   6.___

7. Legumes and nuts provide much
   A. thiamine   B. calcium   C. niacin   D. sodium
   7.___

8. Rich in thiamine is
   A. orange juice   B. cheese
   C. polished rice   D. brewer's yeast
   8.___

9. Carbohydrate stored in the liver is
   A. galleasss   B. glycogen
   C. liepstarch   D. galactose
   9.___

10. The antihemmorhagic is
    A. riboflavin   B. vitamin A
    C. vitamin K   D. niacin
    10.___

11. At the end of one year, the weight of an infant in relation to its birth weight should be
    A. an increase of 12 oz. monthly
    B. double
    C. 20 pounds more
    D. triple
    11.___

2 (#2)

12. Pellagra indicates a deficiency of
    A. ascorbic acid   B. niacin
    C. thiamine   D. riboflavin

13. Provitamin A is
    A. ergosterol   B. carotene
    C. lysine   D. pyrodoxine

14. The nutritionally important minerals are
    A. sodium, iodine, potassium, copper
    B. iron, iodine, phosphorus, calcium
    C. iron, potassium, sulphur, copper
    D. sodium, phosphorus, sulphur, calcium

15. Root vegetables are BEST stored in atmosphere that is maintained
    A. at $36°F$ B. dehumidified
    C. at $30°F$ D. at 75% humidity

16. The government stamp on meats indicates
    A. date when slaughtered   B. point of origin
    C. nutritional value   D. quality

17. Whole grain products, in contrast with enriched products, possess more
    A. hydrocarbons   B. carbohydrates
    C. vitamins   D. proteins

18. In anabolism, the number of calories yielded by one gram of hydrocarbon is
    A. six   B. seven   C. eight   D. nine

19. In the digestion of starch, the intermediate product is
    A. dextrin   B. fibrinogen C. cerine   D. maltine

20. Egg whites whip more quickly at the Fahrenheit temperature of
    A. $0°$ B. $30°$ C. $70°$ D. $85°$

KEY (CORRECT ANSWERS)

1. D		11. D	
2. D		12. B	
3. A		13. B	
4. B		14. B	
5. A		15. A	
6. B		16. D	
7. A		17. D	
8. D		18. D	
9. B		19. A	
10. C		20. C	

EXAMINATION SECTION

TEST 1

DIRECTIONS: Each question or incomplete statement is followed by several suggested answers or completions. Select the one that BEST answers the question or completes the statement. *PRINT THE LETTER OF THE CORRECT ANSWER IN THE SPACE AT THE RIGHT.*

1. The human thyroid requires
   - A. potassium
   - B. carbohydrate
   - C. iodine
   - D. sulphur

2. The passage of dissolved food from the cavity of the alimentary canal into the bloodstream is known as
   - A. assimilation
   - B. anabolism
   - C. catabolism
   - D. osmosis

3. The enzyme which functions ONLY in an acid medium is
   - A. amylopsin
   - B. pepsin
   - C. ptyalin
   - D. trypsin

4. The change of nutrients into protoplasm is called
   - A. anabolism
   - B. catabolism
   - C. karyokinesis
   - D. osmosis

5. Fat is digested MAINLY in the
   - A. gall bladder
   - B. large intestine
   - C. mouth
   - D. small intestine

6. The passage of digested substances into the villi for distribution through the body is called
   - A. absorption
   - B. metabolism
   - C. anabolism
   - D. peristalsis

7. Bile salts are valuable as digestive agents for fats because they
   - A. supply the proper chemical medium
   - B. emulsify
   - C. neutralize
   - D. increase surface tension

8. Flavinoids which are effective in human health are
   - A. biotics
   - B. bioflavinoids
   - C. neoflavinoids
   - D. vitamins

9. Salts which affect the alkalinity or acidity of protoplasm have
   - A. osmotic action
   - B. buffer action
   - C. reduction
   - D. condensation

10. The mineral which maintains osmotic pressure is
    - A. potassium
    - B. sodium
    - C. magnesium
    - D. iron

11. The process of hydrogenation converts
    A. salt water to fresh water
    B. unsaturated fats to saturated fats
    C. fatty acids to cholesterol
    D. cholesterol to fatty acids

12. Amino acids are absorbed MAINLY in the
    A. intestine B. stomach C. pancreas D. liver

13. Uric acid results from
    A. vitamin deficiency
    B. metabolism of purines
    C. digestion of carbohydrates
    D. injection of nicotine

14. An enzyme that produces digestion products which do not set to form a gel is
    A. protease B. bromelin C. diastase D. lycine

15. As a result of the metabolic processes, the body
    A. can form protein from fat
    B. cannot form carbohydrate from protein
    C. cannot form fat from protein
    D. can form carbohydrate from protein

16. Which of the following minerals is found in GREATEST abundance in the human body?
    A. Phosphorus B. Calcium
    C. Iron D. Iodine

17. The enzyme of the gastric juice which aids in the digestion of milk is
    A. trypsin B. amylopsin C. rennin D. ptyalin

18. The digestive enzyme which functions in an acid medium is
    A. pepsin B. ptyalin C. trypsin D. amylopsin

19. Ascorbic acid is less susceptible to oxidation processes when it is
    A. alone B. combined with an alkali
    C. combined with an acid D. thoroughly aerated

20. In weight control, the MOST important reason of the following, for slow increase or decrease of weight is to make sure that the person
    A. is not forced to accept radical changes
    B. changes his eating pattern
    C. is allowed to adjust gradually
    D. avoids digestive upsets

21. During digestion, proteins are reduced to
    A. ascorbic acid B. amino acids
    C. glucose D. glycogen

3 (#1)

22. When water is the chemical that causes changes in nutrients during digestion, the procedure is referred to as
    A. hydrocarbons   B. carbonizing
    C. hydrolysis   D. hydroponics

23. Of the following, the nutrient that does NOT act as a regulator of body processes is
    A. a vitamin   B. fat   C. water   A. a mineral

24. The glands involved in the digestion of starches are the
    A. spleen   B. salivary   C. thyroid   D. adrenal

25. Retarded digestion of cooked protein is caused by
    A. chemical change in the food
    B. physical change in the food
    C. destruction of bacteria
    D. slow cooking in moist heat

26. An important function of protein is to regulate
    A. body temperature
    B. glandular secretions
    C. specific dynamic action of foodstuffs
    D. the buffer action in the bloodstream

27. The normal source of insulin in the human body is the
    A. liver   B. thymus
    C. pancreas   D. pineal gland

28. The pathway of excretion of the nitrogenous end products of protein metabolism is the
    A. lungs   B. skin
    C. kidneys   D. large intestine

29. Carbohydrate stored in the liver is
    A. galleass   B. glycogen
    C. liepstarch   D. galactose

30. Carbohydrates are especially good for
    A. energy and endurance   B. building bones
    C. weight gain   D. Vitamin C

KEY (CORRECT ANSWERS)

1. C	11. B	21. B
2. D	12. A	22. C
3. B	13. B	23. B
4. B	14. C	24. B
5. D	15. D	25. A
6. A	16. B	26. D
7. B	17. C	27. C
8. B	18. A	28. C
9. B	19. C	29. B
10. B	20. B	30. A

TEST 2

DIRECTIONS: Each question or incomplete statement is followed by several suggested answers or completions. Select the one that BEST answers the question or completes the statement. *PRINT THE LETTER OF THE CORRECT ANSWER IN THE SPACE AT THE RIGHT.*

1. The digestive secretion that is acid in reaction is
   A. saliva B. gastric juice
   C. pancreatic juice D. bile — 1.___

2. Enzymes
   A. cause food changes
   B. are activated by boiling
   C. dissolve osmotic membranes
   D. increase reaction at freezing point — 2.___

3. An intermediate product in the digestion of starch is
   A. dextrin B. cerine C. maltine D. fibrinogen — 3.___

4. Amino acids are substances containing
   A. hydrogen B. nitrogen C. oxygen D. carbon — 4.___

5. Digestive secretions of the human body contain chemical compounds called
   A. peptones B. polysaccharides
   C. proteoses D. enzymes — 5.___

6. Amino acids are absorbed through the
   A. stomach B. liver
   C. intestines D. pancreas — 6.___

7. The clotting of blood is aided by
   A. phosphorus B. calcium
   C. iron D. copper — 7.___

8. The mineral that is responsible for the alkaline reaction of the human blood is
   A. calcium B. phosphorus
   C. iodine D. iron — 8.___

9. Digestion of food is helped by having your mealtimes
   A. hurried B. happy C. worried D. exciting — 9.___

10. The alternate contractions and relaxations which constitute the normal beating of the heart are dependent in part upon the presence of _____ salts.
    A. calcium
    B. calcium and sodium
    C. potassium and sodium
    D. calcium, sodium, and potassium — 10.___

11. A catalytic agent that brings about the normal metabolism of carbohydrates in all cells of the body is
    A. insulin B. riboflavin
    C. glucose D. thiamin

12. Vitamin A helps to
    A. give energy
    B. stimulate an appetite
    C. prevent eye and nose infection
    D. aid digestion

13. The body uses calcium for making
    A. scar tissue B. fat
    C. bone D. fingernails

14. A partially complete protein is one which
    A. is capable of maintaining growth but not life
    B. contains all the essential amino acids except glycinine
    C. is capable of maintaining neither life nor growth
    D. is capable of maintaining life but not growth

15. Salts affecting acidity or alkalinity of protoplasm have the effect of
    A. osmotic action B. condensation
    C. reduction D. buffer action

16. An acid ash is yielded by body oxidation of
    A. meats B. citrus fruits
    C. potatoes D. cream

17. The presence of acetone in urine indicates faulty metabolism of
    A. proteins B. carbohydrates
    C. fats D. minerals

18. A vitamin preparation given merely to satisfy a patient is being used as a
    A. dilative B. pacific
    C. placebo D. tranquilizer

19. The organ, the secretion of which neutralizes some poisons and dissolves cholesterol is the
    A. spleen B. thyroid C. pancreas D. liver

20. The PRINCIPAL element which maintains osmotic pressure in the human system is
    A. iron B. potassium C. magnesium D. sodium

21. The nutritive value of a protein is ultimately dependent upon its
    A. digestibility
    B. meat source
    C. connective tissue content
    D. amino acid content

3 (#2)

22. In fever conditions, the basal metabolism of a person as compared to the norm is
A. lower B. higher C. constant D. unchanged

23. Digested food is absorbed MAINLY in the
A. small intestine B. stomach
C. large intestine D. esophagus

24. The digestion of protein is accomplished by the action of the enzymes
A. pepsin, trypsin, erepsin
B. glycerol, lipase, amylopsis
C. lecithin, cystine, lysine
D. glycogen, ptyalin, galactose

25. In comparison with proteins, fats contain LESS
A. carbon B. hydrogen
C. phosphorus D. nitrogen

26. The gland which produces insulin is the
A. spleen B. pituitary C. thymus D. pancreas

27. The process of hydrogenation converts
A. salt water to fresh water
B. unsaturated fats to saturated fats
C. fatty acids to cholesterol
D. cholesterol to fatty acids

28. In the digestion of starch, an intermediate product is
A. dextrin B. fibrinogen
C. cerine D. maltine

29. Amino acids are absorbed MAINLY in the
A. stomach B. liver C. pancreas D. intestine

30. In anabolism, the number of calories yielded by one gram of hydrocarbon is
A. six B. seven C. eight D. nine

KEY (CORRECT ANSWERS)

1. B	11. A	21. D
2. A	12. C	22. B
3. A	13. C	23. A
4. B	14. B	24. A
5. D	15. D	25. D
6. C	16. A	26. D
7. B	17. C	27. B
8. B	18. C	28. A
9. B	19. D	29. D
10. B	20. D	30. D

EXAMINATION SECTION

DIRECTIONS: Each question or incomplete statement is followed by several suggested answers or completions. Select the one that BEST answers the question or completes the statement. *PRINT THE LETTER OF THE CORRECT ANSWER IN THE SPACE AT THE RIGHT.*

Questions 1-50.

DIRECTIONS: For the following group of vocabulary questions, indicate the word or phrase nearest in meaning or most closely related to the first word.

1. Adipose
   A. fatty, fat-like
   B. remedy to allay thirst
   C. glandular
   D. starch hydrolyzer

2. Cortisone
   A. sedative drug
   B. hormone
   C. surface layer
   D. upper part of a tooth

3. Trauma
   A. wound or injury
   B. muscle twitch
   C. fat-soluble substance
   D. sea fishing net

4. Methionine
   A. synthetic vitamin K
   B. amino acid
   C. digestive enzyme
   D. member of the vitamin B complex

5. Viyella
   A. blend of cotton and wool fibers
   B. a clear soup with finely cut vegetables
   C. a water softener
   D. yellow pigment in egg yolk

6. Julienne
   A. opera star
   B. vegetables cut in matchlike strips
   C. exultant joy
   D. iced beverage

7. Chiffonier
   A. chest of drawers
   B. sheer fabric
   C. a hair style
   D. affable, courteous nature

8. Vitellin
   A. vigor
   B. food provisions
   C. compound that relieves vitamin deficiency
   D. a protein in egg yolk

9. Detergent
   A. soap
   B. soap powder
   C. soapless product
   D. any cleaning agent

10. Cabochon
    A. trimming braid
    B. clams
    C. convex cut stone
    D. oysters

11. Pave
    A. a home site
    B. setting for a number of jewels
    C. resistance to *pilling*
    D. water resistant finish

12. Bouillabaisse
    A. highly seasoned fish chowder
    B. hot or cold beet soup
    C. gold braid used on uniforms
    D. ornamental charm against evil

13. One who polishes precious stones
    A. carver
    B. paleolith
    C. lapidary
    D. lithophyte

14. Provencale
    A. French dialect
    B. soup
    C. kind of garnish
    D. type of collar

15. Ricotta
    A. cheese
    B. squash
    C. coloring
    D. colorful fabric

16. Vermicelli
    A. micaceous minerals
    B. bright red pigment
    C. infestation with vermin
    D. a paste-like spaghetti

17. Cochineal
    A. red dye
    B. cotton staple
    C. wool staple
    D. process of dyeing

18. Lipase
    A. digestive enzyme
    B. fat-like substance
    C. anti-oxidant
    D. amino acid

19. Dielectric cookery
    A. braising
    B. cooking in a non-conducting substance
    C. boiling
    D. fricasseeing

20. Catalyst
    A. digestive enzyme
    B. regressive change in tissues
    C. cup-shaped interior of a flower
    D. purgative medicine

21. Keratomalcia
    A. precursor of vitamin K
    B. softening of the cornea of the eye
    C. hardening of the eyeball tissue
    D. inflammation of the tongue

22. Hypovitaminosis
    A. excessive exposure to sunlight
    B. inadequate food supply
    C. excessive vitamin intake
    D. inadequate vitamin intake

23. Glucose
    A. wheat protein
    B. monosaccharide
    C. milk sugar
    D. potato starch

24. Geriatrics
    A. division of a state or county into unfair election districts
    B. heavy use of pungent food seasonings in cooking
    C. prevention and treatment of diseases of old age
    D. fatty infiltration of the blood vessels in old age

25. Friable
    A. capable of painting on wet plaster
    B. capable of being fried in deep fat
    C. simulating Italian pottery
    D. easily broken or crumbled

26. Gliadin
    A. amino acid
    B. end product of carbohydrate digestion
    C. a wheat protein
    D. liver starch

27. Hyperchlorhydria
    A. excessive chlorination of water supply
    B. feverish condition
    C. excessive gastric secretion of hydrochloric acid
    D. excess of cholesterol in the blood

28. Necrosis
    A. spore case
    B. final stage of liver injury
    C. manifestation of iron deficiency
    D. death of tissue

29. Drupe
    A. fruit, e.g., peach
    B. thick, creamy fish soup
    C. narcotic substance
    D. sea anchor

30. Chyme
    A. partially digested food
    B. chopped fish used as bait
    C. pupa of insects
    D. a tendon or nerve filament

31. Roux paste
    A. furniture polish   B. floor polish
    C. cream puff dough   D. tart pastry

32. Provitamin
    A. vitamin conditioning   B. vitamin precursor
    C. biotin   D. vitamin coenzyme

33. Homogenization
    A. reduces bacterial content
    B. reduces fat content
    C. standardizes fat content
    D. reduces size of fat globules

34. Megaloblast
    A. red blood cell   B. synthetic drug
    C. stabilizer   D. mordant

35. Wetzel grid
    A. type of potato pancake
    B. chart used in following development of children
    C. grating used in development of leg muscles
    D. metal claw used on table legs

36. Vitiligo
    A. skin disease   B. pickling compound
    C. abuse   D. giddiness

37. Epigastrium
    A. pelvis   B. abdomen   C. cranium   D. thorax

38. Viable
    A. pellucid   B. easily influenced
    C. capable of living   D. minutely projective

39. Dross
    A. luster   B. dull surface
    C. impurity   D. depression

40. Mete
    A. allot   B. supply with facts
    C. make suitable   D. come up to or touch

41. Taut
    A. stingy   B. hard
    C. shock-proof   D. tightly drawn

42. Viosterol
    A. filterable virus   B. dilated vein
    C. irradiated ergosterol D. infra-red light rays

43. Turgid
    A. muddy   B. insubordinate   C. distended   D. hooded

44. Apartheid
    A. diminution
    B. mitigation
    C. segregation
    D. agreement

45. Desiccate
    A. set apart
    B. divide
    C. dry
    D. destroy in large part

46. Ringworm
    A. coccus bacterium
    B. allergy
    C. fungus
    D. intestinal ailment

47. Pelf
    A. equipment
    B. hide
    C. stolen property
    D. synthetic fur

48. Ketosis
    A. deficiency of vitamin K
    B. increased water retention
    C. inflammation of corneal tissue
    D. incomplete oxidation of fatty acids

49. Astigmatism
    A. far-sightedness
    B. near-sightedness
    C. lack of coordination of eyeball muscles
    D. irregular curvature of the cornea

50. Creole
    A. sauce
    B. cajun
    C. Indian
    D. spice

KEY (CORRECT ANSWERS)

1. A	11. B	21. B	31. C	41. D
2. B	12. A	22. C	32. B	42. C
3. A	13. C	23. B	33. D	43. C
4. B	14. A	24. C	34. A	44. C
5. A	15. A	25. D	35. B	45. C
6. B	16. D	26. C	36. A	46. C
7. A	17. A	27. C	37. B	47. C
8. D	18. A	28. D	38. C	48. D
9. D	19. B	29. A	39. C	49. D
10. C	20. A	30. A	40. A	50. A

BASIC FUNDAMENTALS OF VITAMINS

I. WHAT ARE VITAMINS?

They are a group of organic (carbon-containing) compounds that regulate reactions occurring in metabolism - the process by which the body breaks down and uses foods. Once called accessory food factors, vitamins are necessary because, just as water needs heat to boil, certain processes in the body won't occur properly without vitamins. Scientists don't fully understand why. The most popular theory is that the vitamins serve as traffic controllers, telling the body when certain procedures may begin, or determining speed and duration. Thus, the absence of a vitamin may block a reaction in a cell, thereby disrupting the cell's balance and causing it to form improperly or function abnormally.

Unlike some other organisms, the human body does not manufacture vitamins, and needs to acquire them from diet. Scientists now think that the reason is built in, a result of evolution. In the beginning, the theory goes, simple organisms could get everything they needed straight from the environment. But as life forms became more complex, the ability to make those compounds directly from elements in nature was lost. And in the case of vitamin C, they think that our body's inability to synthesize it is a form of *genetic disease*. That is, we did not discard the ability on the way to becoming *man*, but rather something went wrong in the formation of our metabolic process so that the ingredients we need to make vitamin C are completely missing.

Vitamins are subdivided into two basic classifications - water-soluble and fat-soluble.

Water-soluble vitamins (except vitamin C) serve as catalysts in metabolic activity. They help the body transfer energy from food, and aid in breaking down fats, carbohydrates, and proteins. During digestion, those vitamins are absorbed into the intestine - where no chemical reaction is needed to make them usable - and then pass directly to the bloodstream, where they are carried to body tissues for use. Each of the water-soluble vitamins serves a very special function in the body. For example, vitamins B_1 and B_6 control the conversion of carbohydrates and proteins into metabolic energy (calories), while niacin and riboflavin transport hydrogen during metabolism, thereby causing specific proteins, fats, and carbohydrates to be formed. Vitamin C aids in the formation of collagen, the connective tissue of skin, tendons, and bone, and in absorption and use of iron and potassium. Water-soluble vitamins are not normally stored in the body.

The fat-soluble vitamins are a much more sophisticated group. They serve more highly specialized functions and are much more selectively distributed in nature. They include vitamins A, D, E, and K, all of which can be stored in the body and can be toxic when taken in excess. The fat-solubles are necessary for the synthesis of some body enzymes (substances that speed up or start chemical reactions in the body), and form part of many biological membranes. They are transported by lymph from the intestines to the circulating blood. More fat-solubles than water-solubles are stored in the body, with A, D, and K stored in the liver and vitamin E stored in body fat. Also, since fat is necessary to break down those vitamins, anything that impedes fat metabolism can inhibit their use.

One of the best ways to make sure that your diet is providing your body with what it needs is to make sure that it is varied. It doesn't really matter if you do not savor a few members of any of the basic food groups, since there are enough other foods rich in the same nutrients to take up the slack. You don't have to eat liver to get iron, if you dislike it. Eat spinach in a salad instead and get plenty of iron and some vitamin A too.

Contrary to the faddist notion, the idea of taking each little vitamin in a separate tablet (as opposed to the more common multiple-vitamin tablet) is wrong. What people are doing by this practice is spending a good deal of money and taking the chance of vitamin overdose. It is simply useless to load the body with substances it can't possibly utilize.

In fact, the whole idea of vitamin pills is superfluous unless a person (1) has an illness that eliminates an entire food group from the diet, (2) is the sort of vegetarian who eschews eggs, butter, milk, cheese, and all meats, poultry, and fish, or (3) is pregnant, sick or so poor that a varied, quality diet is impossible. If you are in doubt about your supply of vitamins, ask your physician for advice and take only those prescribed.

Also, people should interpret in a common-sense way the *recommended daily requirement* phrase. This simply refers to an optimum amount that scientists have found to be healthy for humans. One will find that the United States requires one amount, Canada another, and some other country another. This doesn't at all mean that, if you're getting less than this amount of a vitamin, you're deficient.

II. FAT-SOLUBLE VITAMINS

Vitamin	Uses	Possible Results of Deficiency	Possible Results of Surplus	Sources
A (Retinol)	Serves in the formation of normal skin and the mucosa, internal skin, bone, and tooth formation, night and color vision	Deterioration of skin, faulty bone and tooth development, deterioration of eyes, night blindness and blindness	Drying and peeling of skin, loss of hair, bone, and joint pain, fragile bones, enlarged liver and spleen; in severe cases, death	Liver, butter, and fortified margarine, cream, whole milk and cheese made from whole milk, carrots, and dark green leafy vegetables
D	Regulates intestinal absorption of calcium and phosphorus and utilization of those minerals in bones and soft tissue, and plays a part in protein metabolism	In children: delayed tooth development, large joints, soft bones that are easily deformed and broken, deformities of chest, skull, spine, and pelvis (rickets). In adults: osteomalacia (adult rickets), characterized by softening of bones	Weakness, weight loss, vomiting, diarrhea, calcium deposits in soft tissues, kidney damage and death	Formed by direct exposure of skin to sunlight, fortified milk, fish liver oils; also, small amounts of butter made in the summer, liver, egg yolk, and fatty fish like sardines, salmon, and tuna
E	An antioxidant to reduce oxidation of vitamin A, the carotenes, and poly-unsaturated fatty acids	Deficiency (rare and even difficult to produce experimentally) causes mild anemia and destruction of red blood cells	Excess (although there is no conclusive evidence) is believed to cause muscle damage and fatigue	Vegetable oils like cottonseed, safflower, sunflower, soybean; corn, almonds, peanuts, wheat germ, rice germ, asparagus, green leafy vegetables, liver, margarine, vegetable shortening

Vitamin	Uses	Possible Results of Deficiency	Possible Results of Surplus	Sources
K	Necessary for proper clotting of blood	Leads to prolonged clotting time and hemorrhagic disease in newborn infants	Excess of menaquinone, a synthetic form, can cause jaundice in newborn infants, but natural forms have not been found to be toxic. An excess in adults is unlikely.	The main source is synthesis by normal bacteria in the intestine, a function that can be inhibited by some antibiotics. Food sources include lettuce, spinach, kale, cauliflower, cabbage, liver, egg yolk, soybean oils.

III. WATER-SOLUBLE VITAMINS

Vitamin	Uses	Possible Results of Deficiency	Possible Results of Surplus	Sources
C (ascorbic acid)	Aids in the formation of collagen, the connective tissue of skin, tendons, and bone, in the formation of hemoglobin, the absorption and use of iron and phosphorus, and possibly in the metabolism of protein and carbohydrates.	Poor bone and tooth development, bleeding gums, weakened cartilage and capillary walls, skin hemorrhages, anemia (scurvy)	A possible factor in the destruction of vitamin B_{12} in ingested food.	Citrus fruits, tomatoes, cantaloupe, and other melons, berries, green leafy vegetables, peppers, broccoli, cauliflower, and fresh potatoes
B_1 (Thiamine)	Necessary for carbohydrate metabolism	Apathy, depression, poor appetite, lack of tone in the gastrointestinal tract, constipation, heart failure (beriberi)	No known effects	Whole-grain flours and cereals, wheat germ, seeds like sunflower and sesame, nuts like peanuts and pine nuts, legumes like soybeans, organ meats, pork (one of the richest sources)

Vitamin	Uses	Possible Results of Deficiency	Possible Results of Surplus	Sources
B_2 (Ribo- flavin)	Used in enzymes that transport hydrogen in the body as part of the metabolism of carbohydrates, fats, and proteins	Cracks at corners of lips, scaly skin around nose and ears, sore tongue and mouth, itching, burning eyes, sensitivity to light	No known effects	Liver, kidney, cheese, milk, eggs, leafy vegetables, enriched bread, lean meat, beans, and peas
Niacin	Forms part of co- enzymes needed for hydrogen transport and for health of tissue cells	Skin rash, sore mouth and tongue, inflamed membranes in the digestive tract, depression, mental disorienta- tion and stupor (pellagra)	Flushing of skin and occasionally jaundice	Organ meats, lean meats, poultry, fish, wheat germ and whole-grain flours and cereals, nuts, seeds, rice, beans, and peas. The amino acid tryp- tophan can be con- verted to niacin in the body
B_6	Used in metabo- lism of protein, essential for conversion of the amino acid trypto- phan to niacin in the body	Dermatitis around eyes, at angles of mouth, sore mouth and smooth red tongue, weight loss, dizziness, vomiting, anemia, kidney stones, nervous distur- bances and convul- sions	No known effects	Seeds like sunflower, wheat germ and bran, whole-grain bread, flours and cereals, liver, meats, fish and poultry, pota- toes, beans and brown rice
Panto- thenic acid	Essential to many chemical reactions, particularly meta- bolism and release of energy from fat, protein, and car- bohydrates	Unlikely unless a part of total B vitamin deficiency. Unless the diet consists solely of highly processed foods, this defi- ciency is seldom seen	No known effects	Liver, eggs, wheat germ, peanuts, and peas; widely dis- tributed in most foods

Vitamin	Uses	Possible Results Of Deficiency	Possible Results of Surplus	Sources
Biotin	Essential for metabolism of protein, fats, and carbohydrates and energy release	Dermatitis, loss of appetite, nausea, insomnia, deep depression, and muscle pain. Occurs only when large quantities of raw egg whites are consumed over a long period since audin, a protein in raw egg white, blocks absorption of biotin	No known effects	Widely distributed in food, but the best sources are liver, egg yolk, nuts, and legumes
Folacin	Essential for the synthesis of nucleic acids, the building blocks of life	Smooth red tongue, intestinal distress, macrocytic anemia, and failure of young red blood cells to mature	No known effects	Liver, leafy vegetables, dried beans and peas, asparagus and broccoli, fresh oranges, whole wheat flours, breads, and cereals
B_{12}	Synthesis of nucleic acids and the amino acid, aspartic acid	Sore tongue, weakness, weight loss, tingling hands and feet, back pain, mental and nervous changes, eventually pernicious anemia, and irreversible deterioration of the spinal cord	No known effects	Only in animal foods like liver, meats, poultry, fish, and shellfish, eggs and milk and milk products

Glossary of Dietary Terms

CONTENTS

	Page
Absorption ...... Basal metabolism	1
Beikost ...... Catabolism	2
Catecholamines ...... Dietitian	3
Dietitian, Registered (R.D.) ...... Gavage	4
Gelatin ...... Ketogenic-antiketogenic ratio	5
Ketosis .... Micronutrient	6
Microgram ...... Pasteurized	7
Pellagra .... Secretagogue	8
Short-chain fatty acid ...... Vitamin D	9
Vitamin E ...... Zinc	10

Glossary of Dietary Terms

Absorption. Assimilation or taking up of nutrients, fluids, gases, or other substances by the stomach or intestinal walls following digestion.

Acetone (dimethyl ketone). Product of incomplete oxidation of fats. May occur in diabetes mellitus, giving a fruity odor to the breath.

Acid-forming foods. Foods in which the acidic residue exceeds the alkaline residue.

Acidosis. An abnormal increase of acids in the blood caused by accumulation of an excess of acids in the body or by excessive loss of base; characterized by a fall in the pH of the blood or decrease in the alkali reserve in the body. Examples of acidosis include the ketosis (of diabetes mellitus), phosphoric, sulfuric, and hydrochloric acids (of renal insufficiency), lactic acid (or prolonged exercise), and carbonic acid (in respiratory disease).

ADA. Abbreviation for the American Dietetic Association, American Diabetes Association, and American Dental Association.

Adipose. Fat or fatty.

Alcohol. Ethanol. Ethyl alcohol. Distilled from the products of anaerobic fermentation of carbohydrate. An ingredient in a variety of beverages including beer, wine, liqueurs, cordials, and mixed or straight drinks. Pure alcohol itself yields about seven Calories per gram, of which more than 75 percent is available to the body.

Alkaline-forming foods. Foods in which the alkaline residue exceeds the acidic residue.

Alkalosis. An excess of base in the body, commonly resulting from persistent vomiting, excessive sodium bicarbonate intake, or hyperventilation. An abnormal condition of elevated blood pH caused by excessive loss of acids from the body without comparable loss of base or more supply of base than can be neutralized or eliminated.

Allergen. Any agent or substance (usually protein) capable of producing an allergic reaction.

Amino acid (AA). Chief components of proteins. Each amino acid molecule contains one or more amino group ($-NH_2$) and carboxyl group ($-COOH$). Amino acids may be acid, basic, or neutral.

Anabolism. Process of building simple substances into more complex substances.

Anemia. Deficiency in the circulating hemoglobin, red blood cells, or packed cell volume resulting in decreased capacity of the blood to carry oxygen. Macrocytic (large cell size) anemias may result from folacin and B_{12} deficiencies. Microcytic (small cell size), hypochromic (low color index) anemia may result from iron deficiency. Iron, protein, folic acid, vitamin B_{12}, and vitamin C are the major nutrients essential in blood formation.

Anorexia. Lack or loss of appetite for food.

Antibiotic. A substance that destroys or inhibits the growth of bacteria and other micro-organisms.

Antioxidant. A substance which delays or prevents oxidation.

Antivitamin. A substance which may inactivate or destroy a vitamin.

Anuria. Suppression or absence of urinary excretion.

Apatite. Complex calcium phosphate salt giving strength to bones.

Appetite. Natural desire or craving for food.

Arteriosclerosis. Hardening, thickening, and loss of elasticity of the inner walls of arteries and capillaries.

Artificial sweeteners. See saccharin, sorbitol, mannitol, and cyclamate.

Ascorbic acid. Reduced form of vitamin C; water soluble vitamin; prevents scurvy.

Ash. Mineral residue remaining after burning or oxidizing all organic matter.

As Purchased (AP). The weight of food before removing or trimming inedible parts.

Atherosclerosis. A fatty degeneration of the blood vessels and connective tissue of arterial walls. A kind of arteriosclerosis. The fatty deposits, including cholesterol, phospholipids, triglycerides, and other substances, decrease the internal channel size of the blood vessel.

Atony. Lack of normal tone or strength.

Atrophy. A wasting away of the cell, tissue, or organ.

Available. A nutrient that is in a form readily absorbed by the digestive tract and usable by the body.

Avidin. A protein in raw egg white which binds with the B vitamin, biotin, and prevents its absorption from the digestive tract. Cooking inactivates avidin.

Avitaminosis. A condition due to inadequate vitamin intake or absorption, increased body requirement, or antivitamins.

Azotemia uremia. Retention of urea or other nitrogenous substances in the urine.

Balance study. Quantitative method of measuring amount of a nutrient ingested and excreted to determine retention (positive balance) or loss (negative balance).

Basal metabolism. Energy expended at complete physical and mental rest (12-to-16 hours after food ingestion and in thermally neutral temperature). Includes energy for respiration, circulation, gastrointestinal contractions, muscle tone, body temperature, and organ function. Basal metabolic rate (BMR) for an adult is approximately one Calorie per kilogram body weight per hour.

Beikost. Foods other than milk or formula.

Beriberi. Nutritional deficiency of thiamin (vitamin B_1) resulting in loss of appetite, general weakness, progressive edema, polyneuritis, and enlarged heart.

Bile. A fluid produced in the liver, stored, and concentrated in the gallbladder, and emptied into the duodenum to aid in digestion of fat.

Biological value (BV). The efficiency of food protein in supplying amino acids in the proper amounts for protein synthesis in the body. For example, meat has a high biological value (HBV) and beans have a low value. The Thomas-Mitchell equation for calculating BV follows:

%BV = $\frac{100\% \times N \text{ intake} - [(FN-MN) + (UN EN)]}{N \text{ intake} - (FN-MN)}$

where N = nitrogen, FN = fecal nitrogen, MN = metabolic nitrogen, UN = urinary nitrogen, and EN = endogenous nitrogen.

Biotin. A member of the water-soluble vitamin B complex; aids in fixation of carbon dioxide in fatty acid synthesis. Widely distributed in foodstuffs and synthesized by intestinal bacteria. Deficiency may be induced by large amount of avidin, causing scaly dermatitis, muscle pains, general malaise, and depression.

Bland. Any food that is not irritating to the gastric mucosa.

Blood lipids. Primarily cholesterol, phospholipid, and triglyceride which are bound to protein and circulate in the plasma.

Blood sugar level (BSL). The level of glucose (blood sugar) per 100 ml blood.

Bowel. The intestines.

Bran. The outer layer of whole grain. It contains iron, phosphorus, B vitamins, and fiber. Fiber absorbs water, softens and increases the bulk of stools, and facilitates elimination.

Brat diet. Diet consisting of banana, rice, applesauce, and toast; prescribed for diarrhea, especially for infants and children.

Bulk. The indigestible portion of carbohydrates which cannot be hydrolyzed by gastrointestinal enzymes.

Bulking agent. A metabolically inert substance which increases food volume without increasing calories.

BUN. Blood urea nitrogen.

Caffeine. An alkaloidal purine in coffee, tea, and cola drinks. A cardiac and renal stimulant which produces varying pharmacologic responses.

Calciferol. Vitamin D_2. A fat soluble vitamin produced by ergosterol irradiation. Prevents rickets.

Calcium. A major mineral, essential in bone formation, blood clotting, muscle tone, and nerve function. Deficiency may result in rickets or possibly osteomalacia.

Caffeine. An alkaloidal purine in coffee, tea, and cola drinks. A cardiac and renal stimulant which produces varying pharmacologic responses.

Calciferol. Vitamin D_2. A fat soluble vitamin produced by ergosterol irradiation. Prevents rickets.

Calcium. A major mineral, essential in bone formation, blood clotting, muscle tone, and nerve function. Deficiency may result in rickets or possibly osteomalacia.

Calorie. The amount of heat energy required to raise the temperature of one kilogram of water one degree Centigrade. This is the large Calorie, or kilocalorie as used in nutrition. Calories come from carbohydrate, protein, fat, alcohol, and alcohol derivatives (like sorbitol).

Calculus. Commonly called stone.

Carbohydrate. One of three major energy sources in food. Contains carbon, hydrogen, and oxygen. *Available carbohydrates,* such as sugar and starch, provide glucose and glycogen to the body and supply four Calories per gram. *Indigestible carbohydrate* is primarily indigestible plant cellulose.

Carob powder. A powder that looks and tastes like chocolate but does not contain lactose. It may be used as a substitute for chocolate on lactose and galactose restricted diets.

Carotene. Yellow-red plant pigment converted in the body to vitamin A. Two international units of betacarotene are equivalent to one international unit of vitamin A. Abundant in green leafy, and yellow vegetables.

Casein. A milk protein which can contain large amounts of lactose. A phosphoprotein.

Casein hydrolysate. Chemical decomposition of the principal protein of milk.

Catabolism. Opposite of anabolism. Metabolic

process in which complex substances are broken down into simpler substances, usually yielding energy. Destructive metabolism.

Catecholamines. Chemicals synthesized in the brain, sympathetic nerve endings, peripheral tissues, and adrenal medulla.

Celiac disease. Malabsorptive syndrome due to sensitivity to gluten and resulting in decreased jejunal mucosa absorption of fat, carbohydrates, protein, vitamins, and minerals. See Wheat Elimination, paragraph 11–3.

Cellulose. The structural fibers in plants. Indigestible polysaccharide which provides bulk to the diet.

Cholecalciferol. Vitamin D_3. Initiates production of a calcium-binding protein.

Cholesterol. Fat-like steroid alcohol found in all tissues. It may be synthesized in the body, but is usually absorbed from the digestive tract in the presence of fat. It is excreted in bile. Foods of animal origin are dietary sources of cholesterol. It is a key part of the fatty deposits in the arterial wall in atherosclerosis.

Choline. A component of lecithin. Necessary for fat transport, preventing accumulation of fat in the liver. Occurs in all plant and animal cells and may be synthesized from glycine (an amino acid) in the presence of a methyl group.

Chylomicron. A blood lipoprotein containing primarily triglycerides from dietary fat and smaller amounts of cholesterol, phospholipid, and protein.

Chyluria. The presence of a fat globule emulsion, formed in the small intestine after digestion, in the urine giving it a milky appearance.

Clinical nutrition. That branch of the health sciences having to do with the diagnosis, treatment, and prevention of human disease caused by deficiency, excess, or metabolic imbalance of dietary nutrients.

Cobalamin. Vitamin B_{12}. Antipernicious anemia factor; extrinsic factor.

Coffee oils. Possible cause of gastrointestinal irritation, diarrhea is a common symptom.

Colloid. A material whose particles are between 1 and 100 millimicrons in size and dispersed throughout a medium. The particles in dispersion are larger than ordinary crystalloid molecules but are not large enough to settle out under the influence of gravity. Examples are blood protein and gelatin.

Connective tissue. Collagen and elastin. Collagen is converted to gelatin by moist heat cookery. Elastin is not broken down or softened in cooking.

Creatinine. One of the end products of food protein breakdown. The amount excreted in the urine is an index of muscle mass and may be used as a measure of basal heat production.

Clear liquid dessert. Desserts that provide little or no residue, including plain gelatin and Popsicles.

Crystalloid. Small molecules dissolved in a medium such as salt dissolved in water. Other examples are Na^+, K^+, other electrolytes, BUN, uric acid, and creatinine dissolved in the blood.

Curds. The clumped part of curdled milk which contains lactose.

Cyanocobalamin. Vitamin B_{12}.

Cyclamates. A noncaloric sweetener with 30 to 60 times the sweet taste of sucrose. A sodium or calcium salt of cyclohexylsulfamic acid. Cyclamate was changed from the GRAS (generally recognized as safe by the Food and Drug Administration) list to drug status, permitting use only under medical supervision. A suspected carcinogen.

Dehydration. Removal of water from food, tissue, or substrate.

Dehydroascorbic acid. Oxidized vitamin C; biologically active; reversibly oxidized and reduced.

Deciliter. One-tenth of a liter.

Denaturation. To change the chemical, physical, or biologic properties of protein by heating, freezing, irradiation, pressure, or organic solvent application.

Dextrin. The intermediate product of starch breakdown; a polysaccharide.

Dialysis. To separate substances in a solution by using a semipermeable membrane; small substances will pass through and larger molecules will not. As used in food preparation, see attachment 5.

Diet. Food and drink consumed. See specific types in text.

Dietary consultation. Individualized professional guidance provided to assist patients in adapting food consumption to meet health needs. The patient's background, socioeconomic needs, and personal preferences are considered when instructing patients on the physician-prescribed diet.

Dietary history. Record of an individual's food intake taken by 24-hour recall or repeated food records. Basis for individualized dietary consultation.

Dietary status. Bodily condition resulting from the utilization of the essential nutrients available to the body. Dietary history provides some indication of dietary status.

Dietetics. The science and art of planning, preparing, and serving meals to individuals and groups according to the principles of nutrition and management: economic, social, cultural, psychological, and health or disease conditions are considered.

Dietitian. A professional who practices dietetics after following a prescribed academic program for a baccalaureate degree in an accredited institution and completing an accredited internship, or equivalent.

Dietitian, Registered (R.D.). A qualified dietitian who has also successfully completed the examination for professional registration and maintains continuing education requirements by completing 75 clock hours of professional education every 5 years.

Digestibility. The amount of nutrient absorbed by the body and not excreted in the feces.

Digestion. Process of converting food into substances which can be absorbed by the body.

Disaccharidase. An enzyme which hydrolyzes disaccharides to yield two single sugars.

Diuresis. Increased secretion of urine.

Dumping syndrome. Postgastrectomy epigastric discomfort resulting when a large amount of hypertonic, concentrated food draws large quantities of fluid from the bloodstream into the intestine.

Duodenum. The first segment of small intestine between the pylorus and jejunum. Pancreatic juice and bile are secreted into the duodenum.

Edible portion (EP). The trimmed weight of food that is normally eaten.

Effusion. Fluid escaping into a part or tissue.

Endogenous. Originating within the cell or tissue.

Endogenous protein. Body or tissue protein.

Energy. Capacity to do work, such as muscular activity, maintaining body temperature, and operating metabolic processes. As obtained from food oxidation, energy is expressed in calories.

Enrichment. The addition of one or more nutrients to a food to attain a higher level of those nutrients than normally present in the food. Bread and flour are often enriched.

Enteral. Within or by way of the intestine. Often used to refer to supplemental oral, or tube feedings.

Enzyme. An organic compound (usually protein) which accelerates metabolic reactions (such as digestion).

Epinephrine. A hormone released primarily in response to hypoglycemia. It increases blood pressure, stimulates the heart muscle, accelerates the heart rate, and increases cardiac output.

Ergosterol. A plant steroid converted to vitamin D_2, calciferol, upon irradiation or exposure to ultraviolet light.

Essential amino acid. Those amino acids that cannot be synthesized by the body; they must be obtained from food to ensure normal growth, development, and tissue repair.

Essential fatty acid. Fatty acids that cannot be synthesized in adequate amounts by the body to ensure growth, reproduction, skin health, and proper fat utilization.

Ethanol. See alcohol.

Ethylenediamine-tetraacetate. A non-nutritive food additive used to separate a part from a whole, or to act as a metal scavenger.

Exchange list. Grouping of foods similar in nutrients together so they may be used interchangeably.

Excipient. Any addition to a medicine designed to permit proper shaping or consistency.

Exogenous. Originating outside, externally caused.

Extrinsic factor. Vitamin B_{12}.

Exudative enteropathics. Any disease of the intestine with material escaped from the blood vessels deposited in the intestine.

Fat. One of three major sources of food energy, which provides nine Calories per gram. A mixture of glyceryl esters of fatty acids; an oily, yellow, or white substance of animal or vegetable sources.

Fatty acid. Organic acids which combine with glycerol to form fat.

Favism. An acute hemolytic anemia resulting from ingestion of fava beans (horse or broad beans).

Ferment. Chemical change caused by digestive enzymes of micro-organisms.

Fiber. An indigestible part of fruits, vegetables, cereals, and grains important in the diet as roughage, or bulk.

Flatulence. Excessive gas in the stomach or intestines.

Folacin. Folic acid. Pteroylglutamic acid. A water-soluble vitamin of the B complex group needed for normal growth and hemopoiesis. Widely distributed in plant and animal tissues. Deficiency may be induced by sulfonamides or folic acid antagonists.

Food habit. Usual pattern of an individual or group for choosing, preparing, and eating food resulting from family, cultural, economic, and religious influences.

Fortification. The addition of one or more nutrients to a food whether or not they are naturally present. An example is margarine fortified with vitamin A.

Full liquid dessert. Desserts that are fluid or that easily become fluid, including plain gelatin, ice cream, soft custard, and pudding.

Galactose. A six carbon monosaccharide.

Galactosemia. Galactose in the blood due to an inborn error of metabolism in which the enzyme galactose-1-phosphate uridyl transferase is absent; thus, galactose is not converted to glucose. Mental and growth retardation, liver and spleen enlargement, cataracts, jaundice, weight loss, vomiting, and diarrhea result unless dietary modification eliminates lactose- and galactose-containing foods from the diet.

Gavage. Feeding via insertion of a tube through the mouth into the stomach.

Gelatin. An incomplete protein obtained from partial hydrolysis of collagen.

Geriatrics. Study and treatment of diseases and problems occurring in old age.

Glomerular filtration rate (GFR). Milliliters of blood which pass through the kidney glomeruli in one minute; may be used to estimate kidney function.

Glucose. Dextrose. Grape sugar. Blood sugar. A monosaccharide which may be absorbed into the bloodstream and is the major source of energy for the brain and nervous tissues.

Glutathione. A tripeptide believed to assist sulfhydryl containing enzymes to stay in the reduced state essential for their activity.

Gluten. A cereal grain protein; gluten provides elasticity to bread dough.

Glycogen. A polysaccharide composed of glucose units. The main form of carbohydrate stored by man and animals in liver, muscles, and other tissues.

Gram. A unit of mass and weight in the metric system. An ounce is approximately 28 grams.

Gravidity. Pregnancy.

Hemicellulose. A largely indigestible plant polysaccharide that absorbs water. Pectin is a hemicellulose that may lower serum cholesterol. *JADA* 69:501, 1976.

Hemodialysis. Dialyzing blood to remove waste products.

Hepatosplenomegaly. Enlargement of both liver and spleen.

High biological value (HBV) protein. A protein readily digested, absorbed, and utilized by the body, such as the protein in eggs.

Homeostasis. Balance of the internal environment including fluid, pH, body temperature, blood sugar level, heart and pulse rates, and hormonal control.

Hydrogenated oil. Addition of molecular hydrogen to double bonds in unsaturated fatty acids creating saturated solid fat with reduced essential fatty acid biological value.

Hypercholesterolemia. Elevated blood cholesterol associated with cardiovascular diseases.

Hyperchylomicronemia. Elevation of chylomicron lipoproteins circulating in the blood.

Hyperkalemia. Increased potassium in the blood.

Hyperlipidemia. An elevation of one or more lipid constituents of the blood.

Hyperlipoproteinemia. Elevation of blood lipoproteins.

Hypernatremia. Excessive amount of sodium in the blood.

Idiopathic. Without known origin.

Ileum. The part of the small intestine between the jejunum and large intestine.

Inborn error of metabolism. A metabolic defect existing at birth due to missing genes.

Incomplete protein. A protein lacking one or more essential amino acids.

Ingestion. Eating or drinking; taking in.

Inorganic. Minerals that do not contain carbon.

Inositol. A water soluble alcohol found primarily in cereal grains which combines with phosphate to form phytic acid.

Instant cereal. Pregelatinized (precooked) cereal requiring addition of water before serving.

Insulin. A hormone secreted by the beta cells of the islets of Langerhans in the pancreas. It is essential to carbohydrate metabolism in the body. Exogenous insulin is injected by some diabetics to provide proper carbohydrate metabolism.

Insulin shock (or) reaction. Very low blood sugar level resulting from overdose of insulin. Symptoms include hunger, weakness, nervousness, double vision, shallow breathing, sweating, headache, dizziness, mental confusion, muscular twitching, convulsion, loss of consciousness, coma, and eventually death. Fruit juice or intravenous glucose are often used to counteract insulin reaction.

International unit. A measure of biologic activity of a nutrient.

Interpolate. To determine intermediate values in a series based on observed values or to introduce new material in a given subject.

Intrinsic factor. Chemical in gastric juice that facilitates vitamin B_{12} (extrinsic factor) absorption. Lack of intrinsic factor results in pernicious anemia.

Iodine. A trace mineral essential in regulating basal metabolism. Deficiency results in goiter.

Iodine number (or) value. The number of grams of iodine absorbed by 100 grams of fat. Indicates the amount of fatty acids and degree of unsaturation of a fat. The iodine number of saturated coconut oil is 10, and that of polyunsaturated safflower oil is 100.

Iodized salt. Table salt with one part sodium or potassium iodide per 5,000 to 10,000 parts sodium chloride.

Irradiation. Exposure to ultraviolet rays used for destroying microorganisms in food and converting provitamin D to active vitamin D.

Isocaloric. Containing an equal number of Calories.

Jejunum. The part of the small intestine between the duodenum and ileum.

Joule. A metric measure of energy equaling 4.184 Calories.

Junket. The precipitated protein of milk casein and fat.

Ketogenic-antiketogenic ratio. The ratio of the

amount of ketogenic factors, such as fatty acids and ketogenic amino acids, to the amount of antiketogenic factors, such as carbohydrates, glucogenic amino acids, and the glycerol of fat.

Ketosis. An accumulation of ketone bodies (betahydroxybutyric acid, acetoacetic acid, and acetone) from incomplete fatty acid oxidation. Uncontrolled ketosis may result in acidosis.

Kosher foods. Foods prepared and served by Orthodox Judaism dietary laws which include: (1) milk and meat are not consumed at the same meal, (2) meat must be slaughtered in a special ordained manner and cleaned (koshered) by soaking in water, salting, and washing, (3) meat from cudchewing, cloven-hooved animals (cows, sheep, goats) may be eaten, (4) finfish may be eaten. No pork or shellfish are eaten.

Kwashiorkor. Severe protein malnutrition in children resulting in retarded growth, anemia, edema, fatty liver, lack of pigment in the hair and skin, gastrointestinal disorders, muscle atrophy, and psychomotor wasting.

Labile. Unstable.

Lactase. Enzyme that splits lactose to glucose and galactose.

Lactate, lactic acid, lactalbumin. Substances related to lactose but which cannot be changed into galactose by the body.

Lacto-ovo-vegetarian. Person subsisting on grains, legumes, vegetables, fruits, milk, and eggs. Meat, poultry and fish are avoided.

Lactose. "Milk sugar." Disaccharide occurring in milk products. Contains one glucose and one galactose group.

Lactose intolerance. Lactose malabsorption due to lactase deficiency. Results in diarrhea.

Lecithin. Phosphatidyl choline. A phospholipid containing glycerol, fatty acids, phosphoric acid, and choline. Involved in fat transport, lecithin is found in many cells, especially nerves. Lecithin synthesis in the body depends upon dietary intake of methyl groups or choline.

Leucine. An essential amino acid with ketogenic properties.

Licorice. Black flavoring extract containing glycyrrhizic acid which, in large amounts, can cause hypertension and hypokalemia.

Lignin. A constituent of crude fiber. An indigestible cellulose. With cellulose, the principal part of the woody plants. Unlike cellulose, lignin can combine with bile to form insoluble complexes which are not absorbed. *JADA*, vol 69, November 1976.

Linoleic acid. Polyunsaturated essential fatty acid with 18 carbon atoms and two double bonds.

Linolenic acid. A nonessential polyunsaturated fatty acid with 18 carbon atoms and three double bonds.

Lipid. Fat or fat-like substances. Includes fatty acids, triglycerides, phosphatides (such as lecithin), terpenes, and steroids (such as cholesterol).

Lipoprotein. A compound consisting of a simple protein and lipid and involved in lipid transport. Types of lipoprotein circulating in the blood include chylomicrons, alpha lipoproteins (high density lipoproteins, HDL), prebeta lipoproteins (very low density lipoproteins, VLDL), and beta lipoprotein (low density lipoprotein, LDL). All are composed of phospholipid, triglyceride, cholesterol, and protein.

Long-chain fatty acid. Fatty acids containing 12 or more carbon atoms, such as stearic (18 carbon) and palmatic (16 carbon) acids.

Low sodium milk. Milk processed by ion-exchange process to remove approximately 90 percent of the naturally occurring sodium. Thiamin, riboflavin, and calcium are also decreased with an increase in potassium.

Lycine. An essential amino acid and the limiting amino acid in many cereal products.

Magnesium. An essential mineral. A cofactor in metabolism.

Malabsorption syndrome. A condition caused by failure of the body to absorb nutrients such as fats, calcium and other minerals, and vitamins. Examples include celiac disease, chronic pancreatitis, sprue, cystic fibrosis, and carbohydrate intolerance.

Malnutrition. Lack or excess of absorbed nutrients resulting in impaired health status.

Manganese. An essential trace mineral.

Mannitol. A partially absorbed sugar alcohol with a sweet taste equal to sugar but with half the calories.

Maple syrup urine disease. Inborn error of metabolism treated with dietary restriction of leucine, isoleucine, and valine.

Marasmus. Severe protein-calorie malnutrition of infants and young children.

Medium chain fatty acid. Fatty acids containing 8 to 10 carbon atoms, such as caprylic (8 carbon) and capric (10 carbon) acids.

Medium chain triglyceride (MCT). A fat composed primarily of saturated fatty acids with 8 to 10 carbon atoms. A commercially prepared food product for persons not able to digest or absorb food fats and oils.

Menadione. A synthetic vitamin K_3 is much more potent biologically than vitamin K.

Metabolism. Chemical changes in the body; anabolism and catabolism.

Methionine. An essential amino acid important in protein and fat metabolism.

Methylcellulose. Indigestible polysaccharide which provides bulk and satiety without calories.

Micronutrient. Nutrients present in less than

0.005 percent of body weight, such as trace minerals. Also, nutrients present in very small amounts in food.

Microgram. A metric system unit of mass representing one one-millionth of a gram or one one-thousandth of a milligram.

Milk-alkali syndrome. Ingestion of large quantities of milk and alkalies resulting in hypercalcemia, calcium in soft tissues, vomiting, gastrointestinal bleeding, and high blood pressure.

Milliosmole. One thousandth of an osmole.

Mineral. Inorganic elements that build and repair body tissue or control body functions. The ones known to be essential to man are calcium, chlorine, chromium, cobalt, copper, fluorine, iodine, iron, magnesium, manganese, molybdenum, phosphorus, potassium, selenium, sodium, sulfur, and zinc.

Mineral oil. Liquid petroleum substance which is not absorbed by the gastrointestinal tract but interferes with absorption of fat soluble vitamins.

Monosaccharides. Carbohydrates composed of single simple sugars that cannot be hydrolyzed (broken) into smaller units. Examples are fructose, galactose, glucose, and ribose.

Monounsaturated fat. Fat that neither raises nor lowers blood cholesterol. Examples are olive oil and peanut oil.

Monounsaturated fatty acid. Fatty acids with only one unsaturated double bond.

Monosodium glutamate (MSG). A sodium-containing flavoring used in Asian cookery.

Nasogastric tube. Used in tube feeding; a tube inserted via the nose and esophagus into the stomach.

Nausea. Stomach discomfort with a tendency to vomit.

Negative nitrogen balance. Daily nitrogen excretion greater than nitrogen intake which may be brought about by fever, surgery, or burns.

Niacin. Nicotenic acid. A water-soluble B complex vitamin. Antipellagra factor. Necessary to cell respiration, carbohydrate and protein metabolism, and lipid synthesis; thus, requirement varies with caloric intake.

Niacin equivalent. The sum of nicotinic acid and niacin is the niacin equivalent. Sixty milligrams tryptophan may be converted to one milligram nicotinic acid.

Nicotinic acid. Niacin.

Nitrogen balance/equilibrium. An individual is in nitrogen balance when the nitrogen intake from food protein each day is approximately equal to the nitrogen loss in feces and urine.

Non-nutritive sweetener. A noncaloric synthetic sugar substitute. Examples are saccharine and cyclamate.

Norepinephrine. A hormone released primarily in response to hypotension to raise blood pressure.

Nutrient. Any chemical substance useful in nutrition for providing heat and energy, building and repairing tissues, and regulating life processes.

Nutrition. The study of food in relation to health. Combination of processes by which the body receives and uses the materials necessary for body functions, energy, growth, and tissue renewal.

Nutrition history. Laboratory and clinical findings, and a dietary history.

Nutritional status. The condition of the body resulting from consumption and utilization of nutrients.

Nutriture. Tissue nutrient balance of supply and demand.

Obesity. Fat. Body weight approximately 20 percent or more above desirable weight due to adiposity.

Oil. A lipid that is liquid at room temperature.

Oleic acid. An 18 carbon monounsaturated fatty acid abundant in fats and oils.

Oliguria. Decreased urinary output in relation to fluid intake.

Oral hypoglycemic agents. Orally administered compounds that stimulate beta cells in the islands of Langerhans of the pancreas to secrete endogenous insulin that reduces blood glucose in diabetics. Contraindicated for some patients.

Osmolality. A property of a solution which depends on the concentration of the solute per unit of solvent.

Osmolarity. A property of a solution which depends on the concentration of the solute per unit of total volume of solution.

Osmole. The standard unit of osmotic pressure.

Overweight. Fat. Body weight approximately 10 to 20 percent above desirable weight due to adiposity.

Oxalate. Salt of oxalic acid. When combined in insoluble calcium salts, oxalate renders calcium unavailable for absorption.

Pancreatic juice. A digestive juice produced by the pancreas and secreted into the duodenum; contains enzymes involved in digestion of protein, carbohydrate, and fat.

Pantothenic acid. A water-soluble B complex vitamin that is part of coenzyme A. It is essential for growth, normal skin, nervous system development, and adrenal cortex function.

Papain. A proteolytic enzyme of papaya often used as a meat tenderizer.

Parenteral feeding. Food provided without use of the mouth and digestive tract, such as intravenous feeding.

Pasteurized. Heat treated to kill most pathogenic microorganisms. For example, pasteurized eggnog prevents the potential of salmonella infection from eggnog made with raw eggs.

Pellagra. Multiple B vitamin deficiency, notably of niacin. Symptoms include dermatitis, diarrhea, dementia, and death.

Peristalsis. Alternate contraction and relaxation of the gastrointestinal tract which moves contents toward the anus.

Pernicious anemia. Chronic macrocytic anemia due to B_{12} and intrinsic factor deficiency.

pH. A measure of acidity and alkalinity.

Phenylalanine. An essential amino that may be converted to tyrosine. It can be ketogenic, glycogenic, and participate in transamination.

Phenylketonuria (PKU). Inborn error in metabolism resulting in the lack of the enzyme phenylalanine hydroxylase. Phenylalanine cannot be converted to tyrosine without this enzyme. The resultant high levels of phenylalanine result in permanent mental retardation and poor growth and development unless there is close dietary control of phenylalanine ingestion.

Phosphorus. An essential mineral.

Polysaccharide. A complex carbohydrate containing more than four monosaccharides. Examples are glycogen, starch, and cellulose.

Polyunsaturated fatty acids (PUFA). Fatty acids with more than one unsaturated bond in the molecule.

Polyunsaturated: saturated fatty acid ratio (P/S ratio). The relative amount of polyunsaturated linoleic acid to total saturated fatty acids.

Positive nitrogen balance. Nitrogen intake exceeds nitrogen output, such as during infancy and childhood (tissue anabolism).

Potassium. An essential mineral of the intracellular fluids.

Pressor agent. Any substance that raises blood pressure.

Protein. The primary structure of plant and animal bodies. It is composed of amino acids and is approximately 16 percent nitrogen. Protein provides four Calories per gram.

Protein hydrolysate. A mixture of "predigested protein" in the form of amino acids and polypeptides. Used for oral or parenteral feeding in cases of impaired digestion, such as pancreatic diseases.

Protein calorie malnutrition. A condition of severe tissue wasting, subcutaneous fat loss, and dehydration caused by inadequate protein and calorie intake.

Protein quality. A *complete protein* contains all the essential amino acids for growth and life. A *partial protein* maintains life but not growth. An *incomplete protein* can support neither growth nor life. If two incomplete proteins each supply the limiting amino acid(s) of the other, together they may be capable of supporting growth and life.

Protein-sparing. Refers to calories supplied by carbohydrates and fat. These calories save protein from being "burned" as energy so it may be used for anabolism.

Provitamin. A substance related to a vitamin but with no vitamin activity until it is converted to the biologically active form.

P/S ratio. Ratio of polyunsaturated to saturated fatty acids.

Pureed. A food blenderized to a paste consistency. Most baby foods are pureed.

Purine. Nitrogenous compounds of dietary or endogenous origin catabolized to uric acid in the body.

Pyridoxine. An alcohol form of vitamin B_6, a B complex vitamin.

Quick-cooking cereal/rice. Cereals and rice that have disodium phosphate added to reduce their preparation time.

Raffinose. Trisaccharide containing glucose, galactose, and fructose. It is found in beets, roots, underground stems, cottonseed meal, and molasses.

Recommended (Daily) Dietary Allowances (RDA). Suggested amounts of nutrients to provide when planning diets. Designed to maintain good nutrition in healthy persons of average build and activity in a temperature climate with a margin of safety 10 to 50 percent above normal dietary requirements.

Reconstitute. To restore to the normal state, usually by adding water.

Refuse. Inedible, discarded foodstuffs.

Residue. Amount of bulk remaining in the digestive tract after digestion and absorption.

Retinol. A vitamin A alcohol.

Retinol equivalent (RE). Unit expressing vitamin A activity. One RE = 1 u retinol, 6 u beta-carotene, and 12 u for other provitamin A carotenoids.

Riboflavin. Vitamin B_2. Heat stable, water soluble vitamin essential to the health of skin and eyes.

Rickets. Vitamin D deficiency or disturbance of calcium-phosphorus metabolism.

Saccharin. A noncaloric artificial sweetener 700 times sweeter than sugar.

Salt. Table salt; sodium chloride; NaCl.

Satiety. Sense of fullness or comfort; gratification of appetite.

Saturated fat. A fat with no double bonds; chemically satisfied. Often solid at room temperature and usually of animal origin. Examples are butter, lard, and steak fat.

Scurvy. Vitamin C deficiency disease resulting in swollen bleeding gums, hemorrhage of the skin and mucous membranes, and anemia.

Secretagogue. An agent that stimulates secretion.

Short-chain fatty acid. Those containing four to six carbon atoms, such as caproic (6 carbon) and butyric (4 carbon) acids. Yields only about 5 Calories per gram.

Skinfold measurement. Measurement of the thickness of skin at body sites where adipose is normally deposited. Measured with a caliper and compared against a standard chart, it provides an estimate of degree of fatness.

Sodium. An essential mineral important in extracellular body fluids and in regulating many body functions.

Soft. Any easily digested food that is soft in texture and provides no harsh fibers or connective tissue.

Sorbitol. A sugar alcohol apparently metabolized without insulin. It contains 4 calories per gram and can be converted to utilizable carbohydrate in the form of glucose. Excessive use may cause gastrointestinal discomfort and diarrhea.

Specific dynamic action. Increased metabolism from heat of digesting, absorbing, and metabolizing food. Approximately 30 percent for protein, 13 percent for fat, and 4 to 5 percent for carbohydrate.

Standard of identity of foods. Standards established by a government agency, primarily the US Food and Drug Administration, to define quality and container fill for foods.

Stachyose. Tetrasaccharide containing glucose, fructose, and two molecules of galactose. It is found in tubers, peas, lima beans, and beets.

Starch. Plant storage form of carbohydrate (just as the animal storage form is glycogen). A complex polysaccharide. Food sources include breads, cereals, and starchy vegetables.

Sucrose. Table sugar. A disaccharide composed of glucose and fructose.

Sugar. Sucrose. A sweet, soluble carbohydrate that provides 4 Calories of energy per gram.

Sulphur. An essential mineral.

Supplement. A concentrated source of nutrients, such as vitamins or minerals.

Supplementary feeding. Food provided in addition to regular meals to increase nutrient intake.

Sweetening agent (or) sweeteners. Natural sweeteners, such as sugar, or synthetic sweeteners, such as saccharin.

Synthesis. Putting elements together to form a whole.

Tea tannin. Possible cause of constipation.

Textured vegetable protein. Vegetable protein that is flavored, colored, and textured to resemble meat and poultry products.

Theobromine. The alkaloidal stimulant in cocoa beans, tea leaves, and cola nuts that acts as a diuretic, arterial dilator, and myocardial stimulant.

Thiamin. Vitamin B_1, a B complex vitamin and part of a coenzyme important in carbohydrate metabolism. Prevents beriberi.

Threonine. An essential amino acid.

Tocopherols. An alcohol-like group of substances. Four forms have vitamin E activity.

Tofu. Soybean curd; usually available in oriental grocery stores.

Trace minerals. Minerals required by the body in minute amounts.

Triglyceride. A fat composed of a glycerol molecule with three fatty acids.

Tryptophane. An essential amino acid. May be converted to niacin, and a source of the vasoconstrictor serotonin.

Tyramine. A decarboxylation product of tyrosine found in fermented cheeses, wines, and other foods. Produces severe hypertensive reaction if consumed in conjunction with monoamine oxidase inhibitory drugs. See paragraph 8-4.

Underweight. Body weight 10 percent or more below the established standards.

Unsaturated fatty acids. Those with one or more double bonds. Abundant in vegetable oils.

Urea. Major nitrogen containing product of protein metabolism and chief nitrogenous constituent of the urine.

Uremia. A toxic condition caused by the retention in the blood of urinary constituents including urea, creatine, uric acid, and other end products of protein metabolism.

Vasopressor. Any agent that causes contraction of the muscular tissue lining the arteries and capillaries.

Vegetarian (or) vegan. Person subsisting entirely or in a large part on fruits, grains, legumes, and vegetables. If eggs, fish, meat, milk, and poultry are totally excluded, a vegetarian diet may be deficient in calcium, phosphorus, riboflavin, and vitamins B_{12} and D. Pure vegetarian diets are usually inadequate in protein for children.

Viosterol. Vitamin D_2, a product of ergosterol irradiation.

Vitamin. Organic substance provided in minute amounts in food or endogenuously synthesized. Essential in metabolic functions.

Vitamin A. Fat-soluble vitamin necessary for normal skin and bone development, maintenance of vision, and synthesis of mucopolysaccarides.

Vitamin B complex. Water soluble vitamins often found together in nature. Vitamins B_1 (thiamin), B_2 (riboflavin), B_6 group (pyridoxine, pyridoxal, and pyridoxamine), B_{12} group (cobalamins), nicotinic acid (niacin), pteroylglutamic acid (PGA, folacin, or folic acid), pantothenic acid, and biotin. All except B_{12} are coenzymes.

Vitamin C. Water-soluble vitamin. Ascorbic acid.

Vitamin D. Fat-soluble vitamins including ergocalciferol (D_2) and cholecalciferol (D_3).

Vitamin E. Fat-soluble vitamin. Tocopherols.

Vitamin K. Fat-soluble vitamin consumed in food and produced endogenously by intestinal flora. Necessary for blood clotting.

Water. A major nutrient required by the body. Endogenous water is provided as a byproduct of metabolism. Exogenous water may be in the fluid form or contained in food.

Water requirement. Water functions by removing body heat and urinary excreta. One milliliter water per calorie is usually sufficient unless there is a pathological condition such as fever or burn.

Whey. A clear, watery liquid remaining when milk curdles. It contains lactose, but little or no fat.

Zanthine. Weakly basic alkaloid chemicals including caffeine, theophylline, and theobromine.

Zinc. An essential trace mineral involved in growth, digestion, and metabolism. Deficiency results in retarded growth, delayed sexual maturity, and delayed wound healing.